PAUL: A GUIDE FOR THE PERPLEXED

PAUL: A GUIDE FOR THE PERPLEXED

TIMOTHY G. GOMBIS

t &t clark

Published by T&T Clark International
A Continuum Imprint
The Tower Building, 11 York Road, London SE1 7NX
80 Maiden Lane, Suite 704, New York, NY 10038

www.continuumbooks.com

British Library Cataloguing-in-Publication Data
A catalogue record for this book is available from the British Library

ISBN: 978-0-567-03393-2 (Hardback)
          978-0-567-03394-9 (Paperback)

Library of Congress Cataloging-in-Publication Data
A catalog record for this book is available from the Library of Congress.

Typeset by Newgen Imaging Systems Pvt Ltd, Chennai, India

For Mom and Dad, whose lives and loves wonderfully
and faithfully embody the Kingdom of Jesus,
whom Paul preached.

CONTENTS

PREFACE

I have written this book to reflect its title. It is, literally, a guide for the perplexed. I have attempted to provide something of an advanced introduction to guide readers through the complex and complicated issues surrounding Paul, an Apostle of Jesus Christ, a figure whom we encounter in the pages of the Christian canon. It is *a guide*; not *the definitive guide*. I do not attempt to identify and outline a wide range of competing interpretations on every debated issue in Pauline studies. This book represents mainly my own "take" on Paul, though I hope that the advanced student of Paul, along with those who participate in what we call "Pauline scholarship," will recognize in these pages a fair representation of general notions in Pauline studies.

This book is also a guide *to Paul* in that I have left it to others to introduce the debates and histories of interpretation. I will focus mainly on the texts of Paul's letters in this book, noting the general contours of various debates, but engaging primarily and almost exclusively with Paul himself.

Finally, this book is a guide *for the perplexed* in that it seeks to make sense of Paul for those who have spent some time studying his letters, or have read about him in the Book of Acts, the New Testament document that purports to be something of a history of the first Christian generation.

The general field of biblical studies is littered with introductions to the study of Paul, many of them excellent and exceedingly helpful. This is, at first glance, a cause for near paralysis for anyone attempting to write what might be regarded as simply another basic guide to studying Paul. What more needs to be said about him?

Yet, I regard the flood of wonderful introductions as a blessing. Because so many basic issues have been covered by scholars far more qualified than I, and from a variety of perspectives and with an impressive array of approaches, the present guide can be set free to explore more advanced issues and controversies in the letters and "thought" of Paul. Further, while this is not a book of "collected studies," we can be free to explore some issues that are not typically covered in an "introduction."

Because of our situation in what we might call a "postmodern" context—or simply from a desire to be honest and forthright—I must say a word or two about my angle of approach to Paul. I am an orthodox Christian person who, so far as I know, eagerly and fearlessly embraces a critical approach to studying Paul. I regard the New Testament text as Christian Scripture that witnesses to the work of God in Jesus Christ to redeem and transform creation. I do not regard this commitment as in any sense incompatible with a critical engagement with the text of the New Testament, nor incommensurate with a critical posture toward the history of interpretation, both within and without the Christian church through the ages. I locate myself humbly within the stream of Christian readings of Paul and I am grateful for my teachers. I also constantly keep in mind the observation of the great German New Testament scholar Ernst Käsemann, that the history of Pauline interpretation is the story of the church's domestication of Paul. How easy it is to make Paul say what we want him to say!

To my mind, faithful engagement with Paul involves a critical posture toward inherited theological frameworks, testing them by the texts they claim to interpret. It also requires a critical vision of our own prejudices, both in contrast to, or in sympathy with, such inherited frameworks. Finally, we must also subject scholarly consensuses to thoroughgoing scrutiny since such things, having removed "naïve traditional readings" from the interpretive altar, often metamorphose into sacred cows themselves.

All this is to say that the present book is a guide for the perplexed, representing my own read of Paul, though informed by a familiarity with scholarly discussions. Like most other books in this series, I will not engage at length with the work of other scholars, preferring to focus on the texts of Paul's letters themselves, along with an occasional reference to the Book of Acts. For those looking for an introduction to the range of scholarly perspectives in the study of Paul, I can do no better than to commend the excellent work by David Horrell, *An Introduction to the Study of Paul* (2nd edn). Students may also read with great benefit the recent introductory works by Jouette Bassler, Michael Gorman, Magnus Zetterholm, and Michael Bird. My bibliography at the end is not nearly exhaustive, but contains a list of works to which I make reference and which readers may consult who desire further study of the issues I discuss. I have used the SBL Handbook of Style throughout. I have also used the NRSV version for Scripture notations.

I wrote this book during the summer of 2009, supported by a faculty summer grant from Cedarville University. I am grateful for this kind investment in my work. My thanks also go to Frank Plummer, Don Humphreys, Sean Ewing, Chris Miller, Jerry and Kathy Davis, and Leon and Kathy Gombis, who read and commented on earlier drafts of these chapters.

I dedicate this book to my parents, Leon and Kathryn Gombis.

CHAPTER 1

INTRODUCTION

The Apostle Paul is one of the most well-known figures from the ancient world, and certainly the most well-known from the first Christian century. He is the popularizer of the Christian faith, the one who brought it to a wider audience. The Christian movement, at least for its first generation, was almost strictly Jewish, based in and around Jerusalem. Paul is responsible for "internationalizing" Christianity. What is surprising upon closer inspection is that a number of other figures were more prominent during the first century itself—Christian leaders such as Peter, James, and Barnabas. But we have a greater fund of letters from Paul than from anyone else of that era, and he appears as one of two major actors—the more prominent, actually—in the story told by Luke in the Book of Acts. Paul is commonly regarded as the first Christian "thinker," the one who reflects at greatest length on the meaning of Jesus Christ for the world.

We have quite a literary deposit, then, from this early Christian leader. Many of these texts are loaded with emotion, written by someone who does nothing to hide the effects of relational stress. Paul's letters are not dispassionate treatises on abstract notions that relate little to the realities of life in this world. He resonates across the centuries, affecting readers in ways that few authors have done. Herein lies the blessing and curse. The great Cambridge Pauline scholar Morna Hooker is known to open her lectures on Paul with the following: "The problem with Paul is that we know too much about him. Or, at least we think we do." Familiarity has bred misunderstanding and wildly divergent interpretations. Because Paul wears his heart on his sleeve, as it were, and because his triumphs and struggles are laid bare for all to see in the pages of the Christian canon, many people throughout the ages have used Paul's words to interpret and articulate their life experiences and religious journeys. Paul is, at once, both tantalizingly near to us and frustratingly foreign to us.

1 PAUL IN THE CHRISTIAN CANON

Paul did not write a Gospel. We do not have Paul's "take" on Jesus Christ in the same way that we would had he written either one of the four canonical gospels or a work similar to them. Paul wrote letters. This is important in that we know very little of how Paul conceived of Jesus other than how he thought contingently about how communities of Jesus-followers ought to look. The "logic" of the Christian Canon involves the fourfold apostolic testimony to the reality and identity of Jesus (Matthew, Mark, Luke, John), along with a narrative account of significant aspects of the first Christian generation (the Book of Acts). Paul's letters follow.

In the Western churches, the narrative accounts of Jesus are interpreted, to a significant degree, through categories supplied by the interpretation of Paul. The great Apostle gives us theological or conceptual categories through which to understand the four Gospels. Paul has become the chief interpreter of Jesus Christ and of the Christian God, even though he did not compose any of the four narrative accounts of Jesus Christ. This is a default canonical reading strategy for most Christians, though it is far from preferable. It likely stems from the fact that Paul writes in what appears to be easily understood language that appeals immediately on a visceral level.

2 HOW WE KNOW HIM

Paul very likely never contemplated being known by generations after him. He would not have thought about himself as a figure with any sort of a legacy, much less a literary one. He never sat down to write his memoirs, nor did he leave us with autobiographical notes designed to be turned into a work of appreciation and reflection. Had he done so, we would have something very different from his letters. In this sense, Paul is a figure quite unlike Alexander the Great, Cicero, or Julius Caesar. All that we know of Paul is embedded in the cut and thrust of live situations and often quite heated relationships. We know about Paul from seeing him in action, but only *part* of the action. We know Paul, and we know *about* Paul, from two main sources: his letters and from the Book of Acts, Luke's narrative account of the first Christian generation. We will discuss each of these in turn.

2.1 Paul's letters

There are 13 letters in the New Testament attributed to Paul. These are, for the most part, one half of two-sided conversations between Paul and churches he founded. Scholars make educated guesses as to the nature of the other sides of these conversations, but we just cannot be as sure as we often imagine. A further complication is that while these 13 letters are all attributed to Paul, the majority opinion of scholars is that only seven of them are *certainly* written by Paul. The authorship of the remaining six letters is disputed.

Genuine Letters	Disputed Letters
Romans	Ephesians
1 Corinthians	Colossians
2 Corinthians	2 Thessalonians
Galatians	1 Timothy
1 Thessalonians	2 Timothy
Philippians	Titus
Philemon	

The reasons why some of these letters are regarded as not genuinely from Paul vary from scholar to scholar and from generation to generation. One major factor is that the style of the disputed letters differs from that of the undisputed letters, and this has to do with both vocabulary and grammar. For example, in Galatians and Romans, Paul has much to say about "justification by faith," relationships between Jews and gentiles, and God's righteousness. These are major concerns to Paul with regard to salvation. In stark contrast to this, the letter of Ephesians never mentions "justification," but has much to say about "salvation." Further, the sentence constructions in Ephesians are strikingly different from a letter like Galatians or 2 Corinthians. Such stylistic differences might indicate a different author.

Second, differences in theological reasoning point to different authors. In 1 and 2 Timothy, there is a highly developed church structure, with deacons and bishops, and lists of widows. In few other places does Paul mention any sort of church structure, indicating that the "real Paul" regarded church leadership as arising organically and naturally from communities that were animated by the Spirit of God. Such a highly developed church structure indicates that these letters, along with the letter to Titus, were written long after the death of Paul, perhaps even near the beginning of the second century CE. Further, in Colossians and Ephesians, along with the "Pastoral Letters" (1 and 2 Timothy, Titus), social relations are quite "conservative," with gender relations being more hierarchical. Similarly, Colossians and Ephesians say nothing about outlawing slavery. In fact, they call on slaves to submit to their masters, an apparently clear surrender of the radical nature of the genuine Paul's social teachings in Galatians. In that letter, Paul claims that in the Christian community ethnic and gender distinctions are no longer relevant: "There is no longer Jew or Greek, there is no longer slave or free, there is no longer male and female; for all of you are one in Christ Jesus" (Gal. 3:28).

Many believe, therefore, that letters such as Ephesians and the Pastorals represent a reaction against the radical social teachings of Paul. According to a common reconstruction, followers of Paul realized that the early Christian movement would have attracted too much unwanted hostile attention if it continued to press for a more "advanced" social ethic. This is why the genuine Paul's social egalitarianism was either downplayed or reversed outright in the "later" post-Pauline letters.

The disputed letters are, therefore, regarded as "pseudonymous," written by an author other than the named author—written under a "false name"—most likely by a devoted follower of Paul. Pseudonymity, so the claim goes, was widely accepted in the ancient world, even though it strikes modern sensibilities as dishonest and, therefore, unacceptable. It was the common practice for students of a great thinker to perpetuate their master's legacy after his death, or to apply his thought to new contingencies, addressing unforeseen situations in his name. This is the case with the "disputed" Pauline letters—they are written by authors other than Paul in Paul's name either to extend his thought or to address situations that had arisen since his death.

My own sense is that each of the letters attributed to Paul was written or dictated by him and that claims for pseudonymous authorship are unconvincing. I do not hold this position out of a desire to maintain a sense of integrity for the Christian canon, nor do I regard this necessarily as a "conservative" position. It is only that I find the reasoning that drives this consensus view to lack compulsion. Here is what I mean.

It is not really the case that pseudonymity was common in the ancient world, nor do we find analogous situations in the ancient world to that of the disputed Pauline letters. What I mean is that we do find pseudonymity in the Jewish tradition when an author will write under the name of a long-deceased epic figure, such as Enoch, to disseminate his own views. The strategy at work in such cases is quite transparent, with the author spinning a tale of an experience of Enoch to make a contemporary point. The analogy in Paul's case does not fit, since Paul has only recently died and an actual situation is being addressed by someone other than Paul using Paul's name. In his letters, Paul is not publishing treatises for wide dissemination but communicating directly with church communities, even though, as it happens, his letters were distributed throughout the Mediterranean region.

This is far different from anyone using Enoch's name, a figure from the very far distant past in the Scriptures of Israel. No one who encountered 1 Enoch in the first century CE would have regarded it as having come from the actual Enoch. As I said, the literary strategy is transparent. At the same time, no sympathetic Christian encountering 1 Timothy in the first century would have thought that it was not from the actual Paul to the actual Timothy.

There is very little evidence of a disciple of a great thinker writing under that person's name after his death in order to perpetuate his thought. Such an undertaking would be recognized and regarded as unethical. There is evidence of students re-writing the work of the great thinkers whose thought they were studying, but this was primarily for educational purposes. Further, Paul did not found a "school of thought," nor was he necessarily an epic figure apart from what he became long after his death. A final consideration about pseudonymity is that the later church councils made quite penetrating and persevering investigations into the authorship of letters they approved as canonical. If they had found evidence that suggested that Ephesians, for example, was not actually written by Paul, this would have been taken very seriously and that letter would not have been on the approved list of works used in Christian worship.

The lack of any evidence from the ancient world that the letters attributed to Paul were not genuinely from him ought to throw serious doubt on the division between "disputed" and "undisputed" Pauline letters.

Regarding the factors of style and theological reasoning, it is perfectly reasonable to assume that Paul utilized different vocabulary, grammar, and writing style to address different situations. The criterion of style variation is notoriously unstable, since it rules out all of Paul's letters. If we compared Galatians and 1 Corinthians, two letters that scholars assume were surely from the hand of Paul, they vary in style, vocabulary, grammar, and content just as much, if not more, than Galatians or 1 Corinthians do from Ephesians or Colossians. The very simple consideration that Paul wrote in a variety of styles at different times and to different audiences is a far more satisfying conclusion than to submit a proposal that is more difficult to reconcile with what we know from the first century.

As a simple exercise along this line, review four or five of your recent emails from your "sent" box. Look at one to your close friend, one to your boss, one to your spouse, and one to your mother-in-law. Imagine that someone reading these emails 1,500 years from now must determine whether all of the emails come from the same person. Note the variations in subject matter, grammar, style, and vocabulary. You may have written cryptically to your spouse about what you are going to have for dinner, while to your mother-in-law you have written glowingly of your last visit to her house and how well the kids are doing in school, along with how well-behaved they are. This might not harmonize with your email to your close friend, in which you gripe about your mother-in-law and about your oldest son who is actually struggling to get along with your spouse. Not only do these items of correspondence contradict, but the "tone" in each is so different that they surely come from different authors!

Finally, with regard to differences in theological reasoning, it is again unfair to rule out Ephesians because Paul does not mention justification by faith. He discusses this in Romans and Galatians, while we do not find justification by faith making a prominent appearance in 1 Thessalonians, 1 Corinthians, or 2 Corinthians, yet these letters are accepted as genuine.

What has happened in Pauline studies is something that is familiar in scholarship more generally. A consensus has developed over the last two hundred years that has taken on a life of its own. The relegation of six of Paul's letters to "disputed" status has been assumed for so long that to question this consensus is to swim against an overwhelming current. Scholars have grown so accustomed to thinking in these terms that to think otherwise is simply unimaginable, even though the reasons that brought about this way of thinking in the first place (certain understandings of Paul and the nature of the early church) have been undermined or dismissed as outdated, for the most part. Differences of opinion on this issue will not affect much of what we have to say about Paul throughout the rest of this book. It is sufficient for now simply to note the manner in which Paul's letters are regarded by New Testament scholars.

All this is to say that we know Paul from letters he wrote in answer to very specific situations and to address certain problems. We do not have "Paul's thought" in the abstract—apart from concrete situations. That is, we do not have, for instance, "Paul's view of marriage," though Paul does indeed address this topic in several places in his letters. But each discussion is situated *in a context*. We have a record of what Paul said to the church in Corinth on marriage, but his words there appear to be tailored to meet the needs of a very specific contingency about which we do not have much information. In that instance, Paul counsels young men not to marry. If this were the only document we had from Paul, we might say that Paul is "anti-marriage." Paul's "position" on marriage is that it is not good, and that young men ought to refrain from marriage. That, however, does not work across the Pauline corpus, because in a few other places, Paul reacts strongly to the notion that an ascetic lifestyle is commendable (e.g., Col. 2:16–23). Further, in 1 Tim. 4:3–5, Paul says, in response to those who forbid marriage and the enjoyment of good food, that this is an absolute misunderstanding of the character of God and of what God expects from humanity.

2.2 The Book of Acts

Our second source is the Book of Acts, written by Luke. This account of the early Christian movement from about 30 CE to around 60 CE follows the drama of the early years of the Christian mission in Jerusalem, focused around the Apostle Peter and other leaders, such as James and Barnabas. Luke records Paul's conversion (called Saul at that time) in chapter 9 and then takes up exclusively with Paul in chapter 13 through to the end of the book. Scholars, again, have reservations about placing full confidence in all that Luke has to say about Paul in that Luke does not say a word about Paul being a letter writer, nor does he say much by way of criticism of Paul. Further, the speeches recorded in Acts are very obviously highly reworked versions of what must have been said in the actual events. Nor was Luke present to hear most of these speeches.

This does not, however, rule out Luke's story of Paul for our consideration. Much of what we can broadly sketch about Paul, his life and his aims, along with how he reasoned, makes good sense when we compare Luke's account and Paul's letters. Paul's preaching and speeches in Acts cohere well when read in connection with what he says in his letters. In the end, there is very little reason to doubt the historical reliability of Luke's account, broadly speaking. We will, then, take it at face value, noting that what we find in the pages of Luke's account is just that—Luke's account of things. The alternative is to search hard for potential inconsistencies and propose all sorts of impossible-to-prove theories as to Luke's motives, but the series within which the present book is set calls for me to be a guide for the perplexed, not a perplexing cynic!

All of this is just to say that we do not have the sources necessary for a thorough biography in the modern sense. But such is the case with many figures from the ancient world. In our case, we must recognize that we know Paul from his letters, correspondence that is both *situational* and *one-sided*. And almost all of what we know about Paul's life we know from the account written by his friend and traveling partner Luke. We do not have many more sources than these, but we are happy to work with what we have.

3 PAUL'S LIFE

Before he was known as "Paul," he was called "Saul," and hailed from Tarsus, a city in Southeast Asia Minor, modern Turkey (Acts 21:39). Saul was likely born sometime within the first decade of the Common Era (ca. 1–10 CE) to a Jewish family. He inherited Roman citizenship (Acts 16:37–38; 22:25–29; 23:27) and trained as a Pharisee, being sent to Jerusalem to complete his education under Gamaliel (Acts 22:3). His own testimony is that he had a unique zeal and passion for the traditions of his people and for the honor of Israel's God (Phil. 3:6; Gal. 1:13–14; Acts 22:3–5). Because of this, he claimed to have surpassed his contemporaries as he advanced "in Judaism" (Gal. 1:14).

3.1 Saul the Pharisee

As a Pharisee, Saul had membership in a unique group, strongly compelled by the hope of the resurrection from the dead and fulfillment of God's promises to Israel (Acts 23:6; 26:6). These are not what we might term merely "religious" views. They are strongly political and cosmic convictions. Saul, as we will discuss later, was not a "religious" thinker concerned with cultivating the "inner life" for those involved in a range of other pursuits. The Pharisaic hope was in the God of Israel fulfilling the promises to set Israel free from the oppression of the nation's enemies and to restore Israel to its rightful place as God's chief agent of salvation and rule over creation. The aim of the God of Israel was to restore all of creation and to install Israel as the throne from which God ruled over the nations.

Because of this, Israel's current condition—dominated and horribly oppressed by Rome—was intolerable. It needed to be set right. This desperate need set the agenda for the Pharisees. As Saul read the Scriptures of Israel, therefore, he understood that the nation had been sent into exile for unfaithfulness to their God, for idolatry, for neglecting the Mosaic Law and its practices. The calculus was clear. If unfaithfulness to the Mosaic Law led to exile, then renewed faithfulness to the Law *at the national level* would surely move God to act on behalf of Israel to deliver the nation from its enemies and bring about salvation.

So Saul's aim as a Pharisee was to bring about a renewed nation, to present to God a purified people, newly zealous for the Law, every bit as passionate as Saul for the "traditions of the fathers" (Gal. 1:14). He was likely convinced that once the nation was pure and obedient, God would be moved to send Messiah who would bring God's salvation.

And "salvation," for Saul, would have had national, international, and cosmic dimensions. God would bring about *national* renewal, sending God's own Spirit in fulfillment of the promises through the prophets to give life to the nation and renew every Israelite to the life-giving knowledge of God. This would set Israel in its proper place *internationally*. Israel would finally take its place as God's choice nation, teaching, judging, and shepherding the nations on God's behalf, leading them to the worship of the one and only true God, the Most High God over all the nations. Finally, God's salvation was *cosmic* in scope, because God's supra-human enemies—Satan, Sin, Death, and the powers and authorities that oppress creation in the present evil age—would finally be defeated and destroyed.

Saul's aims as a Pharisee, therefore, involved intense involvement in a national campaign for the honor of the God of Israel, advocating for faithfulness to the Mosaic Law. After all, there was much at stake: God will renew all of creation when the nation presents itself to God as a purified people. This is what Paul, years later, has in mind when Luke quotes him in Acts 23:6 saying that he still regarded himself a Pharisee, passionate for the "resurrection from the dead." While this was redefined after his conversion, Saul's entire life was devoted to seeing the promises to the fathers fulfilled. This provided the drive for the Pharisaic passion for purity and holiness.

3.2 Saul and Jesus

We do not have any record of an encounter by Saul with Jesus, though it is likely that Saul knew about him and perhaps even saw and heard him at some point. There were a number of self-appointed "Messiahs" roaming the Judean countryside at this time, occasionally heading into Jerusalem to test their claims, credentials, and abilities at leading a movement of revolt and renewal. Most of these enterprises ended in the death of the supposed Messiah and the stamping out of the attached movement. The terribly efficient and ruthless Roman forces had a low tolerance for revolutionary fervor. That there was an additional such person named "Jesus" would not have been a surprise to Saul.

The death of Jesus, of course, confirmed to Saul that this Jesus was *most certainly not* the Messiah of Israel, especially because of his death *on a Roman cross*. After all, the expected trajectory of any messianic figure was set, to a great degree, by the career of Judas Maccabeus, along with the many figures of deliverance from the Scriptures of Israel, such as Phinehas (Num. 25:7–13; Ps. 106:28–31). These epic figures from the past, among others, informed the popular imagination to expect a violent overthrow of the Romans and the initiation of sustained peace and prosperity. A purported Messiah's death ended all hopes and typically sent followers looking for someone else.

In Gal. 3:13, Paul cites Deut. 21:23, that "cursed is everyone who hangs on a tree." Saul would have contemplated Scripture's (and, by extension, God's own) verdict on Jesus: he was cursed by God, rejected as Messiah. That a movement would have sprung up around this person was blasphemous and intolerable, since it could only be characterized as complete disobedience to the God of Israel, rejecting God's own verdict on Jesus and his claims. For Saul, such a movement was a mortal threat to his fundamental Pharisaic aims and ambitions—Christians were standing in the way of God fulfilling the promises to the fathers! He could not afford to ignore this movement or maintain any kind of neutral posture toward it.

It is no surprise, then, that Saul's first appearance is at the murder of Stephen, recorded in Acts 7:58–60. Luke portrays Saul watching over the coats of those putting Stephen to death after his speech to the council (Acts 7:2–53), giving hearty approval (Acts 8:1). A wave of persecution against the church immediately follows this event, in which Saul plays a leading role. So great was his zeal that he traveled around Judea, "breathing out threats and murder" (Acts 9:1) in attempts to "destroy the church of God" (Gal. 1:14). He must have developed quite a reputation as a persecutor of the church, since after his conversion it was difficult for him to gain any entrée with the first generation of Jesus-followers.

3.3 Convert

As Acts 9 opens, Saul is on his way to Damascus to continue his persecution. On the way, he is confronted by the risen and exalted Jesus, who calls to him from heaven:

> [Saul] fell to the ground and heard a voice saying to him, "Saul, Saul, why do you persecute me?" He asked, "Who are you, Lord?" The reply came, "I am Jesus, whom you are persecuting. But get up and enter the city, and you will be told what you are to do." The men who were travelling with him stood speechless because they heard the voice but saw no one. Saul got up from the ground, and though his eyes were open, he could see nothing; so they led him by the hand and brought him into Damascus. For three days he was without sight, and neither ate nor drank. (Acts 9:4–9)

Saul then went in to Damascus, meeting with Ananias, a Christian whom God had told to inform Saul of his new commission. Saul was appointed to bring the gospel of Jesus Christ to the gentiles and, in anticipation of one of the main features of the future apostle's ministry, was to be told "how much he must suffer for the sake of [Jesus'] name" (Acts 9:16).

After spending 3 years in Arabia (Gal. 1:18), most likely in and around Damascus and his home town of Tarsus, Saul traveled to Jerusalem to try to establish relations with the first disciples of Jesus in that city (Acts 9:26). The reception was, to say the least, frosty. The first disciples did not trust Saul. Barnabas, however, served as an envoy and brought Saul to the church. Luke records that "Barnabas took him, brought him to the apostles, and described for them how on the road he had seen the Lord, who had spoken to him, and how in Damascus he had spoken boldly in the name of Jesus" (Acts 9:27).

Saul then tried to initiate his apostolic ministry in Jerusalem but very quickly became a lightning rod for controversy (Acts 9:28–30). Because of a threat to his life, he then went back to his hometown of Tarsus, where he most likely spent the next 10 years. We have no record of what Saul might have been doing during these years.

At some point in 44–45 CE, the Jerusalem church sent Barnabas north to Antioch in Syria to look after the church that had sprung up in that city (Acts 11:22). Soon after arriving there, Barnabas went to Tarsus to search for Saul to recruit him as a ministry associate in Antioch (Acts 9:25–26). A year later, a prophet named Agabus came to Antioch from Jerusalem and predicted a harsh famine, one that would apparently have a devastating affect on the church in Jerusalem. The Antioch church gathered provisions and sent a gift "to the elders by Barnabas and Saul" (Acts 11:30). This visit—Saul's second since his conversion—likely took place around 46 CE and is probably the visit Paul refers to in Gal. 2:1–10.

3.4 First mission

Luke opens up a new chapter of his account in Acts 13 (ca. 47–48 CE) by reminding us of Saul's status at this stage in his career. Luke lists the ministers in Antioch before reporting a prophetic utterance that led to Saul's first recorded mission journey into Asia Minor:

> Now in the church at Antioch there were prophets and teachers: Barnabas, Simeon who was called Niger, Lucius of Cyrene, Manaen a member of the court of Herod the ruler, *and Saul*. While they were worshipping the Lord and fasting, the Holy Spirit said, "Set apart for me Barnabas and Saul for the work to which I have called them." Then after fasting and praying they laid their hands on them and sent them off. (Acts 13:1–3)

If we place Saul's conversion at around 33 CE, then nearly 15 years later, we find a few interesting items. First, our man is still being called "Saul." Many imagine that the change in names comes immediately after his conversion: "Saul" is his pre-Christian name and he is called "Paul" afterward. Somewhat surprisingly, this is not the case. Second, quite late into his career Saul is not at all a major player in the first Christian generation and not even the main figure in the church in Antioch. He is listed after Barnabas, Simeon, Lucius, and Manaen. We might translate the tone of Luke's opening of this scene as follows: "Oh right, there's also this guy called Saul."

In early 47 CE, then, Saul accompanies Barnabas on a mission into Asia Minor. It is during this journey that two important transitions take place. During an encounter with a magician named "Bar-Jesus," Saul seizes the initiative and confronts him in an arrestingly direct manner (Acts 13:10–11). In the midst of this episode Luke begins to refer to him no longer as Saul, but as Paul (13:9). Further, this episode functions for Luke as the hinge point at which Paul becomes the focus of the narrative of Acts. Luke introduces the subsequent episode, in v. 13, in this way: "Then Paul and his companions set sail from Paphos . . ."

On this initial journey, Paul and his companions reached as far west as the city of Perga, which is just a bit less than 250 miles west of Paul's hometown of Tarsus in Asia Minor. On this journey, Paul and Barnabas found several churches, including the church to which he sends his first extant letter, Galatians. This church may have been in the near vicinity of Lystra, where Paul was dragged from the city, stoned, and left for dead (Acts 14:19). This would have left Paul in an unimaginably terrible physical state, possibly with broken bones and

PAUL: A GUIDE FOR THE PERPLEXED

misshapen skull, which may have accounted for his stay in the town to which he sent the letter we know as "Galatians." In pleading with them, Paul says this:

> Friends, I beg you, become as I am, for I also have become as you are. You have done me no wrong. You know that it was because of a physical infirmity that I first announced the gospel to you; though my condition put you to the test, you did not scorn or despise me, but welcomed me as an angel of God, as Christ Jesus. What has become of the goodwill you felt? For I testify that, had it been possible, you would have torn out your eyes and given them to me. (Gal. 4:12–15)

Paul and Barnabas returned home to Antioch late in 48 CE (Acts 14:26–28).

3.5 Controversy

It is at this time that we are introduced to the controversy that more or less defines the remainder of Paul's career—the tension created by the inclusion of the gentiles (non-Jews) in the Christian movement, which was almost entirely Jewish at this point, at least in Jerusalem. At some point late in 48 or early 49 CE, the Apostle Peter made a visit to Antioch. According to Paul's account in Galatians 2, Peter was enjoying the "freedom" of the gospel of Jesus Christ, the freedom of Jews to fellowship fully and freely with non-Jewish Christians (Gal. 2:11–12). The unity inherent in the Christian gospel was embodied through joint table-fellowship, with Jews and non-Jews eating together. This would have offended Jewish convictions about the nature of their food laws.

Very soon after Peter had arrived, some Jewish Christians came from Jerusalem. These very likely were some ultra-conservative Jewish Christians who found it very difficult to imagine that non-Jews could be included in the people of God along with Jewish Christians. Non-Jews could indeed become Christians, but they could only do so by being circumcised and following the Law of Moses. They must convert to Judaism. Their presence had quite an intimidating effect on Peter and Barnabas, who were led into hypocrisy, failing to act "consistently with the truth of the gospel" (Gal. 2:14).

They began holding themselves aloof from the gentiles, refusing to sit and eat with them, maintaining by their actions that gentiles must indeed become Jews in order to share in salvation.

It is likely to this controversy that erupted in Antioch that Luke refers in Acts 15:1–2, a controversy that caused "no small dissension and debate" between Paul and Barnabas and the visitors from Jerusalem. Because of the confusion, the church designated Paul and Barnabas to travel to Jerusalem to discuss the matter with the apostles and elders to get an authoritative ruling on it.

On the way to Jerusalem, Paul received a report of the goings-on in Galatia. Apparently a group very similar to that which had caused trouble in Antioch had made its way to southern Asia Minor and was advocating that the Christians there needed to convert to Judaism to enjoy salvation in Jesus Christ. This series of events likely accounts for the blistering tone of Paul's first letter, which opens with anathemas and curses (Gal. 1:8, 9), and contains some of the bluest language in all of the New Testament. He writes in Gal. 5:10–12:

> But whoever it is that is confusing you will pay the penalty. But my friends, why am I still being persecuted if I am still preaching circumcision? In that case the offence of the cross has been removed. I wish those who unsettle you would castrate themselves!

Paul arrives in 49 CE for what has been called the Jerusalem Council (Acts 15:4). It is likely that even at this point, 16 years after his conversion, Paul was not regarded warmly by the leaders in the Jerusalem church. As the traveling party was making its way through Phoenicia and Samaria, their reports of the conversion of the gentiles "brought great joy to all the believers" (Acts 15:3). When they arrive in Jerusalem, however, they give a similar report and any rejoicing is conspicuously missing from Luke's account. There was doubtless quite a bit of tension directed toward Paul by the more conservative elements in the Jerusalem church. Further, after Peter advocates for the welcome of gentiles into the Christian movement—a glorious exit from the stage of Acts for the great Apostle—Luke records that "the whole assembly kept silence, and listened to *Barnabas and Paul* as they told of all the signs and wonders that God had done through them among the Gentiles" (Acts 15:12). It is not Paul who takes the lead here, but Barnabas, since he was a known commodity and dearly loved by the community in Jerusalem. After James gives the ruling, concluding the council, Paul and Barnabas return to Antioch (Acts 15:30).

3.6 Second mission

Very shortly after returning to Antioch, Paul set off on his second journey, taking him farther west into Macedonia and then south into Greece. Paul is accompanied on this trip by Silas, one of the prophets who had traveled with Paul and Barnabas to Antioch from Jerusalem after the council (Acts 15:32). Paul had a sharp disagreement with Barnabas over taking Mark along with them on this second journey (Acts 15:37–39). Mark, Barnabas's cousin, had accompanied them on their initial journey but "had deserted them in Pamphylia" (Acts 15:38). We are given no more editorial comments from Luke than this, but it does appear that Mark was not quite up to the challenges presented by traveling with Paul. While we may be tempted to pass judgment on the fragile constitution of Mark, or perhaps his weak faith, it is worth remembering that Paul's missions were far more perilous endeavors than either modern tourists or contemporary short-term missionaries typically experience.

We do know that this rupture did not sever Paul's relationship with Mark beyond repair, however. Paul gives the following instructions at the end of his Colossian letter: "Aristarchus my fellow-prisoner greets you, as does Mark the cousin of Barnabas, concerning whom you have received instructions—if he comes to you, welcome him" (Col. 4:10). Further, at the end of his life, Paul writes this: "Only Luke is with me. Get Mark and bring him with you, for he is useful in my ministry" (2 Tim. 4:11).

Paul and Silas founded several churches on this trip, including one in Philippi, a Roman colony, Thessalonica, where he only spent three weeks, and Corinth, where Paul spent 18 months. The churches in Philippi and Corinth were especially dear to Paul, as evidenced from his warmly personal letter to the Philippians and the intensely emotional Corinthian letters. This journey ends in 52 CE, with Paul landing at Caesarea, traveling to Jerusalem to greet the church briefly (his fourth visit after his conversion), and then returning home to Antioch (Acts 18:22). During this journey, Paul writes the two Thessalonian letters.

3.7 Third mission

Paul's third journey is also his longest. In fact, while we might say that this journey lasts for 5 years, it also never quite ends, since Paul is arrested at its end in Jerusalem and he never returns to Antioch. The mission begins in 52 CE (Acts 18:23) and ends in Jerusalem 5 years later (Acts 21:17). He spends the bulk of his time in Ephesus, totaling 3 years. His intimate and very warm relationship with the Ephesian church explains his very emotional farewell to the Ephesian elders in Acts 20:17–38. This is also why most scholars regard the letter of Ephesians as a circular letter, since it is by far his most impersonal epistle. During his Ephesian ministry, Paul also conducts an intense round of correspondence with the Corinthian church, with whom he had spent 18 months during his second journey. Two of these letters survive in the Christian canon, but it is likely that there was at least one further letter sent from Paul, and possibly a total of four.

The following reconstruction assumes that Paul sent the Corinthians four letters. Early in his third mission, Paul sends a letter from Ephesus, referred to in 1 Cor. 5:9–11 (52/53 CE). After Paul hears back from the Corinthians, he sends the letter we know as 1 Corinthians, again from Ephesus (54 CE). Paul then makes a second visit to Corinth, which goes badly (2 Cor. 2:1; 12:14, 21; 13:1–2). This visit likely takes place sometime in 54 CE. Paul then writes a very stern letter (2 Cor. 2:3–4, 9; 7:8, 12), sent from Ephesus and delivered by Titus (2 Cor. 2:12, 13; 7:5–16). This letter is lost to us, but was likely sent sometime early in 55 CE. After some sort of reconciliation takes place, Paul then writes our 2 Corinthians, sent from Macedonia (2 Cor. 7:5; 8:1–5; 9:1–4), and delivered by Titus and two others (2 Cor. 8:17, 18, 22). Luke records a final visit by Paul to Corinth from Macedonia, which lasted three months (Acts 20:1–3; Rom. 16:23; cf. 1 Cor. 1:14).

While Paul is in Corinth, late in 55 or early in 56 CE, he writes to the church in Rome (which may have been a collection of house churches). The church(es) in Rome had likely been founded by Jewish pilgrims returning from Pentecost in 30 CE, and were initially entirely Jewish. The next two decades, however, had likely seen the conversion of a number of gentiles so that the Christian congregation in Rome was mixed, but with Jewish leadership. In 49 CE, the Emperor Claudius expelled the Jews from Rome. The historian

Suetonius records this in his *Life of the Emperor Claudius*: "Since the Jews constantly made disturbances at the instigation of Chrestus, he expelled them from Rome." This reference to "Chrestus" most likely points to Jewish unrest over the Christian movement in some way and to some degree.

This situation was reversed 5 years later, in 54 CE, with the death of Claudius and the rise of Nero. Whatever the precise trouble, the Christian movement was without its leadership for 5 years, a situation which likely allowed the development of non-Jewish leadership in the churches. The return of the Jewish Christians to Rome likely caused no small amount of tension, probably provoking struggles and disputes over leadership and the character of Christian community life.

While in Corinth, Paul hears of this and writes to the Roman church(es) for two reasons. First, even though Paul has no connection to this church he is the apostle to the gentiles and they are within his sphere of ministry. Second, he is hoping to eventually make it to Spain and is hoping that the Roman church can provide something of a mission base for his journey there (Rom. 15:24).

3.8 Toward Jerusalem

While he is in Ephesus, Paul first mentions his ambition to head to Jerusalem and then to travel to Rome: "Now after these things had been accomplished, Paul resolved in the Spirit to go through Macedonia and Achaia, and then to go on to Jerusalem. He said, 'After I have gone there, I must also see Rome'" (Acts 19:21). In his Gospel, Luke portrays Jesus' ministry as inevitably leading toward Jerusalem, and this statement regarding Paul in Acts is an echo of his Gospel: "When the days drew near for him to be taken up, he set his face to go to Jerusalem" (Luke 9:51).

After traveling through Macedonia and Greece and then back up to Northwestern Asia Minor, the momentum of Paul's movement toward Jerusalem begins to build. He first stops in Miletus, which is about 40 miles south of Ephesus. He did not stop in Ephesus, because he did not want to be delayed (Acts 20:16), nor, we might surmise from subsequent events, did he want to be dissuaded from his intention to go to Jerusalem. While in Miletus, he calls for the elders from Ephesus to join him for a farewell. In the midst of a passionate speech, he says,

And now, as a captive to the Spirit, I am on my way to Jerusalem, not knowing what will happen to me there, except that the Holy Spirit testifies to me in every city that imprisonment and persecutions are waiting for me. But I do not count my life of any value to myself, if only I may finish my course and the ministry that I received from the Lord Jesus, to testify to the good news of God's grace. And now I know that none of you, among whom I have gone about proclaiming the kingdom, will ever see my face again. (Acts 20:22–25)

Luke records their response:

When he had finished speaking, he knelt down with them all and prayed. There was much weeping among them all; they embraced Paul and kissed him, grieving especially because of what he had said, that they would not see him again. Then they brought him to the ship. (Acts 20:36–38)

Paul and his companions—Luke is among them—then make stops in Tyre and Caesarea. In both of these places, the believers plead with Paul not to go to Jerusalem, knowing that his arrival there will cause problems and likely result in serious trouble for Paul. Luke records that prophetic utterances are given in both places to this effect (Acts 21:4–5, 10–14). Despite all of this pleading, Paul eventually makes it to Jerusalem in 57 CE (Acts 21:17), his fifth recorded visit to the city since 33 CE.

3.9 Arrest and imprisonment

Paul's reception by the Jerusalem leaders is in marked contrast to that which occurred eight years earlier at the council in 49 CE. Luke states that "when we arrived in Jerusalem, the brothers welcomed us warmly" (Acts 21:17). The next day Paul, along with Luke, meets with the elders and James, giving them a report of his ministry. "When they heard it, they praised God" (Acts 21:20), but they also inform Paul that his presence in Jerusalem is going to cause problems. There are "many thousands" of Jewish Christians who are "zealous for the Law" and who have been told that on his missions among the gentiles Paul is advocating that Jews no longer circumcise their children and stop observing the customs, practices that amount to "forsaking Moses" (Acts 21:20–21). To avoid any uproar that Paul's presence might cause, the elders counsel Paul to go along with four men who are under a vow: "Join these men, go through the rite of purification with them, and pay for the shaving of their heads. Thus all will know that there is nothing in what they have been told about you, but that you yourself observe and guard the law" (Acts 21:24).

Paul does this, but is spotted by some Jews from Asia who then stir up the crowds and attempt to kill him (Acts 21:27–32). Paul is then arrested by the Romans and sent to Caesarea after a plot against his life is discovered. He spends two years (57–59 CE) in Caesarea and appears before Felix (Acts 24:2–26), Festus (Acts 25:6–12), and Agrippa (Acts 25:23–26:29), before being sent to Rome. He had made use of his Roman citizenship and appealed to have his case heard before Caesar (Acts 25:11). Luke quotes Agrippa as saying that had Paul not made this appeal, he would have been set free, since there is no evidence that he had done anything wrong (Acts 26:32). Paul may have written the Prison Letters during this two-year period (Ephesians, Colossians, Philippians, and Philemon).

3.10 Rome

Paul had desired to see Rome, as we noted above, and Luke records Paul's vision of the exalted Jesus during the early stages of his first incarceration assuring him that he would indeed make it to Rome (Acts 23:11). Now, in 59 CE, he is on his way. After a disastrous journey involving shipwreck and a stay on the island of Malta (Acts 27:1–28:10), Paul arrived in Rome, sometime in 60 CE. According to Luke, Paul spent the next two years in Rome and he ends his account rather abruptly:

> He lived there for two whole years at his own expense and welcomed all who came to him, proclaiming the kingdom of God and teaching about the Lord Jesus Christ with all boldness and without hindrance. (Acts 28:30–31)

The remainder of Paul's life is uncertain, but we might speculate that Paul was released from prison in 62 CE and traveled back through Asia Minor, stopping in Crete and Ephesus, at least. He left Titus on Crete and Timothy in Ephesus, to look after Christian communities that had cropped up in those places. On his way back to Rome, he writes letters to Timothy and Titus (ca. 63 CE). When he gets to Rome, Paul is re-arrested and writes his second letter to Timothy. We do not know precisely when Paul died, but according to Christian tradition, he was beheaded during the reign of Nero.

We also cannot be sure that Paul ever made it to Spain, which had been his ambition. Spain, of course, was the edge of the known world for those living in the ancient Mediterranean region. Clement, bishop of Rome, writing in about 96 CE, says the following:

> Paul also obtained the reward of patient endurance, after being seven times thrown into captivity, compelled to flee, and stoned. After preaching both in the East and West, he gained the illustrious reputation due to his faith, having taught righteousness to the whole world, and come to the extreme limit of the West, and suffered martyrdom under the prefects. (1 Clem. 5)

4 CONCLUSION

We cannot write a full-blown modern biography of Paul, since the literature in which we encounter him is highly personal—his own letters—and closely tied to contingent situations. Further, Paul's letters represent only one side of the conversation. The only other extensive source is the Book of Acts, written by Paul's colleague Luke. What we do have, however, delivers to us an intensely fascinating and compelling figure who has commanded widespread and sustained attention over the last two millennia.

CHAPTER 2

PAUL: THEOLOGIAN, MISSIONARY, OR PASTOR?

Because Paul's letters arguably constitute the most significant source for the various theological traditions of the Christian church, many assume that Paul was Christianity's first theologian. While it may be appropriate to say that Paul reasons theologically or "does theology" in his letters, he is not a theologian of the sort that modern Western people might encounter (in the unfortunate event that any person actually encounters a theologian!). If we were to regard Paul as a theologian in the modern academic sense, this would have a significant impact on how we understood his letters and his thought. First, we might imagine that Paul means to "do theology" in a way that is familiar to us. We envision a professional scholar, freed from the rough and tumble of everyday life and detached from ministry commitments, figuring out and working with complex conceptual systems. These systems must fit together logically and have an overall cohesion, and they or may not have any relevance to everyday life.

Regarding Paul as a theologian in the modern sense may also cause us to isolate the "theological" portions of his letters from his other concerns, and perhaps even to assign greater value to these sections. We may look for where he is addressing "soteriological" issues—matters having to do with the doctrine of salvation—or perhaps pay closer attention when he speaks of "eschatology"—the doctrine of end times or "last things." But this fails to take Paul's letters seriously *as whole letters to churches*, not as theological treatises. When we come to 1 Thessalonians, for example, we find Paul spending four chapters reminding the church of his manner of life while he was among them, expressing his love and concern for them, and solidifying his relationship to them. He spends only a brief paragraph on what may properly be termed "theology," discussing matters of "eschatology." Some scholars focus on this paragraph alone as the point of the letter, but that is to fail to understand that "doing theology" is only one task in Paul's larger vision of his vocation. In Paul's own view, obviously, a healthy relationship to the Thessalonian church and his concern to see them flourishing as a community were vital—perhaps even more important—components of what he was all about.

A further, and very closely related, problem with viewing Paul as an academic theologian is that his "less theological" letters are diminished, such as 1 and 2 Thessalonians and Philemon. These letters are, after all, quite practical, tied up with matters that are strikingly mundane. If Paul is a theologian, then we will tend, with many others, to place a higher value on his letter to the Romans, reading it as a "theological treatise," perhaps even Paul's *magnum opus*, his great work in which the Apostle, near the end of his distinguished career, sits down to reflectively map out his "entire theology" in one document. This is a fairly common understanding of Paul and I will argue in this chapter that it is mistaken. The "less theological" of Paul's letters are no less significant than the "more theological" ones, and the latter are far more pastorally focused than is often recognized.

There is no denying, of course, that Paul is something of a theologian, a profound thinker. Anyone who engages with his letters, along with Luke's portrayal, comes away impressed by Paul's lively and nimble mind. If we have in mind a more pastorally engaged theologian, then we may be closer to the mark. We are on safest ground in seeking to understand how Paul regarded himself and his task, and to watch him at work. When we do this, we will see that Paul is a *herald of the Kingdom of God and of the victory and Cosmic Lordship of Jesus Christ*. This is an intensely *political* vocation, since Paul is proclaiming the emergent reality of a radically new political order— the Kingdom of God—along with an alternative ruler; the crucified, risen, and exalted Jesus. This calling as a herald inevitably involved a *pastoral task*, since Paul's aim was to see the creation and establishment of Kingdom of God communities throughout the world.

After his first mission with Barnabas, Luke notes Paul's desire to "return and visit the believers in every city where we proclaimed the word of the Lord and [to] see how they are doing" (Acts 15:36). Here we see that Paul was not merely an evangelist, at least in the modern sense, merely proclaiming the message and then leaving the work of community-building to others. Further, Paul was neither what we might term a missionary, going only to one place and working for the long-term establishment of a Kingdom of God community. Paul's vocation involved elements of each of these, but was completely unique. He was announcing the arrival of the long-awaited Kingdom of God and its universal impact, affecting both Jews and gentiles. His intention was to see these Kingdom of God communities flourish, knowing that their very existence—their creation and growth—were signifiers of the victory of God and cosmic reign of Jesus Christ. His planned visits were meant to encourage any and all signs of growth, to solve problems, to provide correctives, and to continue to transform the communities' re-imagination of the world as God's good creation transformed by the resurrection of Jesus Christ. In situations where Paul could not make subsequent visits, he wrote letters, which serve as substitutes for his own presence. They carry out and extend Paul's vocation and the tasks inherent in it; heralding the arrival of the Kingdom, shepherding and providing situation-specific counsel, and re-shaping community identity and conduct.

Paul is not, then, a theologian in the academic sense, though we might say that he provides the template for anyone aspiring to that task. Nor are Paul's letters random theological reflections over the course of a career in theological studies. *Paul is a herald of the Kingdom of God, which involves tasks of pastoring and counseling communities that constitute outposts of the Kingdom of God on earth.* This inevitably involves Paul in the theological task of interpreting particular situations in light of the arrival of the Kingdom of God into the world.

In this chapter, I will elaborate on this vision of Paul's identity and vocation, demonstrating from a survey of his letters that they are not primarily works of theology but of pastoral care and community transformation. Each of them flows from his vocation as a herald of the Kingdom of God, interpreting each particular situation in light of the invasion of the reign of God in Christ and providing counsel in light of that reality.

1 GALATIANS

Owing to its great influence on Martin Luther and its role (and Luther's) in the Reformation, Galatians is regarded by many as a work of theology. Luther saw in this letter Paul's excoriation of ecclesiastical authorities who might impose upon the freedom of the human spirit and the standing of any one individual before God. While we might acknowledge the validity of Luther's *theological use* of Galatians to speak powerfully in the sixteenth century, this letter is in the first instance a vigorous pastoral letter written to confront and correct a problem in a particular local setting that is quite unique.

As we indicated in the last chapter, the trouble in this church likely arose because of the arrival of a competing missionary group originating from Jerusalem. Representatives of the very conservative Jewish Christian faction in the Jerusalem church were tracking Paul's travels seeking to make certain that the Christian communities that sprang up in Asia Minor were thoroughly Jewish. They represented the group that had argued at the Jerusalem council that while the conversion of the gentiles was a good thing, it was "necessary for them to be circumcised and ordered to keep the Law of Moses" (Acts 15:5). In Galatia, then, this Jewish group was advocating that the gentile converts of Paul must "Judaize"—they must convert to Judaism, adopting a thoroughly Jewish lifestyle, including the circumcision of all males and the adoption of Jewish food laws and Sabbath observance. As Paul envisions the situation, then, these "agitators" (Gal. 5:10) are claiming that for the Kingdom to truly arrive in Galatia, and for the Galatians to truly enjoy an outbreak of Kingdom life, they must adopt a Jewish way of life. From the report that reaches Paul, the Galatians are considering it.

Paul's aim in this blistering letter is to dissuade the church from taking this course. This is not a theology of the Mosaic Law, nor a discussion of the character of justification by faith, but an attempt to solve a crisis situation. The Kingdom of God outpost in this region is under threat and Paul, the herald of the Kingdom, is going to work to identify the threat, call these Kingdom inhabitants away from a disastrous course, and to elucidate for them how to walk in the truth (Gal. 2:14; 5:7).

Paul's strategy in this letter is to marginalize Jewish identity relative to the new creation people of God in Jesus Christ. It is just one of a number of other ethnic identities. What matters for participation in the Kingdom in Galatia is to live according to the faithfulness of Jesus regardless of ethnic identity. Paul says as much in the following repeated formula:

> For in Christ Jesus *neither circumcision nor uncircumcision counts for anything*; the only thing that counts is *faith working through love* (Gal. 5:6).

> For *neither circumcision nor uncircumcision is anything*; but a *new creation is everything.* (Gal. 6:15)

Jewish and non-Jewish identities are completely irrelevant when it comes to participating in the new creation people of God. The manner in which the Galatian Christians are to inhabit the Kingdom of God—the reality of the new creation brought into being by the power of God—is by faith (in Jesus Christ) working through love and not through the adoption of a Jewish—or any other—way of life. In Gal. 6:16, Paul calls this the "rule" that the Galatians are to follow. Again, he would not normally downplay Judaism, living as a Jew, or his Jewish heritage, but in this specific instance where non-Jews are being pressured to go through the upheaval of taking on a Jewish mode of life in order to be an outpost of the Kingdom of God, Paul argues that to be Jewish or non-Jewish is irrelevant.

Paul explains that this is so because of their inclusion in the death and resurrection of Jesus Christ. Jesus Christ died *to this age* in his death and was resurrected to life by God, initiating that future Kingdom age where death and sin are banished forever. According to Paul's theology of the inclusion of all believers in Christ's death and resurrection, believers have died together with Christ (Gal. 2:20) to this present age and have been raised to share in this new creation life even now, in anticipation of the full enjoyment of this reality in the age to come. Paul draws this out at several key points in Galatians. In his opening greeting, Paul notes that Jesus Christ "gave himself for our sins to set us free from the present evil age" (Gal. 1:4). And in his letter closing, Paul says that through the cross of Christ "the world has been crucified to me, and I to the world" (Gal. 6:14). For Paul, then, the evaluation of people based on ethnicity belongs to this present evil age, so that for all those "in Christ," "there is no longer Jew or Greek, there is no longer slave or free, there is no longer male and female; for all of you are one in Christ Jesus" (Gal. 3:28).

Among the arguments that Paul deploys to solve this crisis is the outrageously challenging paragraph in Gal. 3:10–14. We will handle this in Chapter 5 of this book, but for now it is sufficient to note that it is a mistake to read Paul's statements about the Law, the Mosaic

Law, and Judaism in Galatians as if these represent Paul's "thoughts" on Judaism, Jews, and the Scriptures of Israel. What Paul has in mind in speaking of these things is the threat posed by the rival mission in Galatia and the pressure they are bringing to bear on the newly formed church in that province, claiming that to truly be the people of God they need to take on a Jewish identity. Paul is not theologizing in the abstract about the character of Judaism or of the Mosaic Law. His words are directly related to the issue facing the Galatians.

2 THESSALONIAN LETTERS

Paul had only spent 3 weeks in Thessalonica during his second mission before being driven out of the city, according to Luke's account (Acts 17:1–10). After being sent along to Athens to avoid trouble (Acts 17:15; 1 Thess. 3:1–3), Paul sent Timothy to find out about the converts in Thessalonica. He was worried that they might be persuaded to give up on their new-found faith because of the unrest caused by their conversion. When Paul arrived in Corinth for his extended stay there, Timothy returns to him with a good report (1 Thess. 3:6).

Paul envisions the success of his vocation as vitally connected to the flourishing of new creation communities, which is why he was so eager to find out how the Thessalonians were doing. "For what is our hope or joy or crown of boasting before our Lord Jesus at his coming? Is it not you? Yes, you are our glory and joy!" (1 Thess. 2:19–20). Further, he says, "For we now live, if you continue to stand firm in the Lord" (1 Thess. 3:8). The future evaluation of his ministry before God is directly tied to the flourishing of the communities created through his proclamation. Paul cannot, then, simply proclaim the message and move to another town.

His first letter to the Thessalonians is very tender and filled with reminders of his behavior while he was among them. He did not take advantage of them but worked with his own hands to support himself. He was not there to rip them off.

> As for us, brothers and sisters, when, for a short time, we were made orphans by being separated from you—in person, not in heart—we longed with great eagerness to see you face to face. For we wanted to come to you—certainly I, Paul, wanted to again and again—but Satan blocked our way. (1 Thess. 2:17–18)

The Thessalonians letters are not less significant for our understanding of Paul at all, but reflect Paul's vocation as a herald of the Kingdom of God, eager to see an outpost of Kingdom presence established in Thessalonica. We do not see Paul content to have proclaimed the gospel before moving on to another place. On the contrary, he nurtures this community in the faith, using whatever means at his disposal.

3 CORINTHIAN LETTERS

Paul spent 18 months with the Corinthians on his second mission and, so far as we can tell from his letters, his relationship with this community was emotionally charged. Paul likely wrote more to this church than the two letters that are preserved, but we see here again the contours of Paul's vocation. His aim in writing to the Corinthians is stated in 1 Cor. 1:10: "Now I appeal to you, brothers and sisters, by the name of our Lord Jesus Christ, that *all of you should be in agreement* and that *there should be no divisions among you*, but that *you should be united* in the same mind and the same purpose."

It appears that factions had developed in the community that ran along several lines. First, there appear to be cults of personality, with certain factions claiming loyalty to Peter, Apollos, and Paul (1 Cor. 1:11–12). That Paul had baptized a handful of people during his time in Corinth is being touted as a badge of honor in an attempt to assert ascendancy over others (1 Cor. 1:14–17). Further, rampant selfishness has overtaken the community that manifests itself in several ways. The rich are exploiting the poor, or at least taking pains to avoid opportunities to serve them. Parties to minor disputes are taking their cases to the secular courts rather than seeking the help of the church to bring about reconciliation. And what Paul terms "spiritual gifts" are being exploited to gain superiority or ascendancy over others. Paul fears that the community may well fail, or that their behavior is manifesting the absence of the Kingdom and a complete ignorance of what the gospel entails.

Because of this, these letters display some of the darker tones sometimes required of him in his vocation as a herald of the Kingdom. He issues some very serious warnings. In 1 Cor. 3:16–17, Paul writes that the Corinthian church is a temple of God, a dwelling place of God's Spirit. The "you" in v. 16 is plural in Greek, so that he is referring to the entire community. Just as God dwelled on earth in the tabernacle and the temple in the Scriptures of Israel, so now God inhabits the new creation community by his Spirit. This reality has serious consequences for those who are fostering division in the community. "If anyone destroys God's temple, God will destroy that person. For God's temple is holy, and you [plural] are that temple" (1 Cor. 3:17).

Paul further warns against complacency in 1 Cor. 9–10. Just because the Corinthians have had wonderful experiences and have been uniquely blessed to become an outpost of new creation life, they must never become arrogant or complacent, thinking that they will escape God's judgment because of their privileges. In 1 Cor. 9:24–27 Paul speaks autobiographically before then turning to the Corinthians to drive home the point:

> Do you not know that in a race the runners all compete, but only one receives the prize? Run in such a way that you may win it. Athletes exercise self-control in all things; they do it to receive a perishable garland, but we an imperishable one. So I do not run aimlessly, nor do I box as though beating the air; but I punish my body and enslave it, so that after proclaiming to others I myself should not be disqualified.

Paul knows that even though he is an apostle of Jesus Christ, a herald of the Kingdom of God, if he becomes complacent and fails to persevere in participating in the Kingdom of God through self-discipline and faithfulness, he will fail at the final judgment.

Paul then warns the Corinthians against idolatry (1 Cor. 10:6–7) and putting Christ to the test through sexual immorality (vv. 8–9). The instances he mentions from Israel and from his own life are to be examples to the Corinthians, "on whom the ends of the ages have come" (v. 12). While he does acknowledge that new creation has erupted in Corinth, Paul again warns his readers: "So if you think you are standing, watch out that you do not fall" (1 Cor. 10:12). As he says in 2 Cor. 5:10, "all of us must appear before the judgment seat of Christ, so that each may receive recompense for what has been done in the body, whether good or evil." Everyone must pass through the future judgment and have their lives examined. This ought to bring sobriety to anyone who considers using the Christian community for their own selfish purposes.

Paul's instruction on the Lord's Supper in 1 Cor. 11 appears in a similar context. Many Christians are familiar with the language used in churches to introduce the Lord's Supper as it appears in vv. 23–26 and may even have heard the warning about self-examination in vv. 27–32, but it is worth pointing out that this instruction does appear in the section where Paul is harshly rebuking the Corinthians. Their current practice of the Lord's Supper is not an embodiment of the Kingdom of God. He claims that "when you come together, it is not really to eat the Lord's supper. For when the time comes to eat, each of you goes ahead with your own supper, and one goes hungry and another becomes drunk" (1 Cor. 11:20–21).

The Lord's Supper was designed as a performance of the Kingdom of God. The meal depicted the radically new relationships created by the death and resurrection of Jesus. Those with resources would purchase more than they needed so that they could share with those who had little. And the poor were warmly welcomed to share in the meal and give thanks for God's bountiful provision in Christ. This was a performed parable of the Kingdom, which is Paul's point in 1 Cor. 11:26: "For as often as you eat this bread and drink the cup, you proclaim the Lord's death until he comes." Paul does not say that preaching should follow the meal, but that *the meal is the preaching*—a living parable of the reality of the Kingdom.

The meal had been perverted, however, into an opportunity for those who were rich to share a meal with their wealthy friends and to shove the poor to the margins. They were refusing to embody new creation life, failing to rightly regard the church as the body of Christ and the practices that depict that reality. This is what Paul means by eating the bread and drinking the cup in an unworthy manner (1 Cor. 11:27). The basic problem in Corinth—divisions in the church—is being reflected in the meal, which is a violation against the "body" of Christ. Paul means to use this term ambivalently in 1 Cor. 11:23–34, to refer both to the actual body of Jesus and to the church as the gathered body of the exalted Jesus, a reality actualized by the Spirit. When Jesus died in his human body and was resurrected to new life as a resurrection body, he created by the Spirit a new body called the church. "For all who eat and drink without discerning the body, eat and drink judgment against themselves" (v. 29). "Discerning the body" involves recognition of this richly textured reality and a commitment to the unity of the church, which the Lord's Supper depicts.

This passage is not, then, an abstracted instruction on the Lord's Supper, such as one might find in a church manual, but a rebuke and an exhortation to embody the Kingdom of God rightly by pursuing unity in the community. Paul's discussion culminates in a statement that is often left out of public readings of this text: "So then, my brothers and sisters, when you come together to eat, *wait for one another*" (1 Cor. 11:33).

As a corrective to the rampant selfishness, arrogance, cults of personality, and battles for supremacy in Corinth, Paul offers his own example of humility and the practice of love. The gospel is culturally subversive in that it undermines the dynamics of the perverted world order. "The message of the cross is foolishness to those who are perishing, but to those who are being saved it is the power of God" (1 Cor. 1:18). Because of this, Paul did not come to Corinth with rhetorically powerful displays, but with humility and in weakness. He did this "so that your faith might rest not on human wisdom but on the power of God" (1 Cor. 2:5). In 2 Corinthians, Paul lays out his humiliations and his suffering as signs of the genuineness of his vocation. As his supreme boast, he mentions his narrow escape from Damascus in a basket through the city wall (2 Cor. 11:30–33). Paul's most well-known passage is also intended as a corrective for the community—his beautiful encomium on love in 1 Cor. 13.

Much more could be said about all that is contained in these rhetorically powerful letters, but hopefully this is sufficient to demonstrate that in his correspondence with the Corinthians Paul is vigorously carrying out his commission to see new creation community life firmly established and flourishing. The Kingdom of God is not manifest in displays of power and wisdom, nor battles for supremacy, but in meekness, humility, love, and ministry to the marginalized. Supremely, the Kingdom of God is embodied by a community that is unified, that makes use of all the resources available from a bountiful God and seeks to include all those who may not have anything to offer by way of payment.

4 ROMANS

More than any other of Paul's letters, Romans is regarded as a work of theology. Scholars typically outline this letter according to categories derived from systematic theology, so we have Paul dealing with universal sinfulness in chapters 1–3; justification by faith in chapters 4–5; growth in sanctification in chapters 6–8; the problem of Israel and God's sovereign election in chapters 9–11; and practical Christian living in chapters 12–15. While many scholars do realize that such a perspective is unrealistic, since Paul was not the initiator of the Western tradition of reflective abstract theology that we often make him out to be, most alternative readings of Romans remain largely the same. Paul is still doing theology, except now perhaps there are different emphases or different purposes for Paul laying out his theology for the Christians in Rome. If there is any recognition of an actual practical purpose, it is that Paul is laying out his theological understanding for the Roman church(es) in order to establish his credentials with them. This has the practical purpose of solidifying a mission base in Rome for his eventual goal of reaching Spain with the gospel.

Romans is not, however, a work of abstract theology. It is a situational letter with a pastoral function. That is, Paul writes *this specific letter* to *this particular community* in Rome facing a unique set of problems. Romans is *pastoral* because Paul is dealing with a church in crisis, writing to them to help them understand the causes of their division, to lay out for them the way forward, and to encourage them to pursue unity as the people of God in Christ—an outpost of the Kingdom of God. He says in Rom. 15:15, "on some points I have written to you rather boldly," something which he cannot say if he is merely theologizing in the abstract. This is indeed a bold pastoral letter! Paul names their divisive conduct as sin and uses their slogans sarcastically, strategies he also utilizes in the Corinthian correspondence. This is what I mean when I say that Romans is a pastoral letter.

As we indicated in the previous chapter, the problem in the Roman Christian community had to do with the return of a large number of Jewish Christians to Rome with the death of Claudius in 54 CE. Claudius had expelled the Jews from Rome in 49 CE, allowing the gentile leadership in the house churches to develop and the gentile profile of the churches to flourish. That is, the Jewish character of their social and communal lives diminished greatly. Now, with the return of Jewish Christians to re-populate the churches and synagogues, and to re-take positions of leadership, there are tensions. The Jewish Christians seem to be asserting their priority as the historic people of the God of Israel in an effort to re-establish some position of prominence among the network of churches. They may even have been using slogans such as "to the Jew first and then to the Greek" (cf. Rom. 1:16; 2:9, 10), and trumpeting their claim as "the seed of Abraham." For their part, gentile Christians are emphasizing their priority over the Jews since the gospel has gone out to the nations (cf. Rom. 11:17–24).

In seeking to solve the problem of disunity in the Roman churches, Paul claims that God's wrath comes upon *all* ungodliness and wickedness of humanity (Rom. 1:18), so that both the Jewish and non-Jewish Christian factions in Rome stand in need of salvation by God in Christ. Because *all* are subject to the judgment of God, everyone in Rome—Jewish *and* non-Jewish Christians—who is passing judgment against anyone else stands condemned (Rom. 2:1). At the final judgment, one's ethnic identity will have no bearing on God's verdict. The judgment will be based on one's deeds so that Jews and non-Jews in Rome who are doing good will receive a favorable judgment (Rom. 2:6–7), and any Jews or non-Jews who "are self-seeking and who obey not the truth but wickedness, there will be wrath and fury" (2:8). "There will be anguish and distress for everyone who does evil, to the Jew first and also to the Greek, but glory and honor and peace for everyone who does good, to the Jew first and also to the Greek" (2:9–10). This is all based on the fact that "*God shows no partiality*" (v. 11).

Not only do all Christians (Jewish and non-Jewish) in Rome have an equal need of God, but their acceptance before God has no relevance to their ethnic identity. Salvation comes to *all* who believe, and there is no distinction between Jews and non-Jews (3:22) because *all* have sinned and fallen short of the glory of God (3:23). The boasting of one group over another, therefore, is eliminated, and all attempts to gain ascendance and dominance over another group ought to be jettisoned (3:27). This becomes clear from a reading of Scripture to foster a community of faithfulness rather than reading Scripture to bolster one group's claims over another (3:27).

Paul then makes a very aggressive rhetorical move in v. 29, and it may have drawn gasps from the Jewish Christians listening to this letter read in one of the Roman gatherings. Remember, we are reading a bold pastoral letter. According to Paul, the claim to priority before God by the Jewish Christians amounts to an assertion that to enjoy God's salvation one must take on Jewish identity. Such a claim, for Paul, is the same thing as confessing that the God of Israel is *not the Great King over all the earth,* a denial of one of the fundamental convictions of Israel's faith. On the contrary, says Paul, God is not the God of Jews only, but of *Jews and gentiles,* and salvation is enjoyed not by taking on Jewish identity, but by faith in Christ, regardless of whether one is Jewish or non-Jewish.

In Rom. 5:6–8, Paul again reasons with his readers fairly boldly, providing a further rebuke to any notion of Jewish-Christians' judging of non-Jewish Christians, by noting that participating "in Christ" demands humility. Paul indicates that *everyone* in Rome must consider themselves both "weak" and "ungodly" (v. 6), since if they were already righteous, then there would be no need for Christ to die. But God's love is seen in that Christ died for us while we were "sinners"—another aggressive rhetorical move—indicating that if there are any in Rome who do not consider themselves to be in that category, then they are not among that group for whom Christ died.

In Rom. 6:19, Paul says that if the Christians in Rome present themselves to righteousness instead of to unrighteousness, the result will be *sanctification.* This is not the process of sanctification in Western systematics—the process of Christian growth that the individual undergoes in a traditional "order of salvation." Paul's logic, rather, is that when the church presents itself and all its members as servants of God's cosmic salvation program, it is truly being the people of God—the "set-apart" ("sanctified") people of God who will one day participate fully in the Kingdom of God. When they were slaves of unrighteousness, fostering divisions and destruction in their communities, they were ashamed and there was widespread discouragement in once-flourishing church fellowships. The outcome of that is the death of the community (vv. 20–21). But now that they are freed from sin and enslaved to God, they are deriving the benefit which is *sanctification*—truly life-giving existence as the people of God and the outcome, eternal life. That is, the future of that sanctified community in Rome that is characterized by unity and goodness is full participation in God's glorious future—the Kingdom of God.

We might say that the debate in the Roman fellowships—at least how Paul *conceives of the discussion*—involves the question, What do the people of God look like? What distinguishes them? How do you know who they are? The two rival answers in Rome revolve around ethnicity—Jewish/non-Jewish identity. Paul's answer transcends this discussion and he claims that the people of God are marked off by those who suffer with Christ. God has sent his Spirit to gather us up into himself and to communicate his presence to the church, and his Spirit witnesses "with our spirit that we are children of God" (Rom. 8:16). Paul then reveals what God's true people look like—those who suffer with Christ. "If, in fact, we suffer with him so that we may also be glorified with him" (Rom. 8:17).

Paul then spends several chapters urging the rival groups in Rome to avoid judging one another (Rom. 14:3, 10) and to receive one another gladly (Rom. 14:1; 15:7). The climax of Paul's letter comes in Romans 15, especially in his benediction in Rom. 15:5–8:

> May the God of steadfastness and encouragement grant you to live in harmony with one another, in accordance with Christ Jesus, so that together you may with one voice glorify the God and Father of our Lord Jesus Christ. Welcome one another, therefore, just as Christ has welcomed you, for the glory of God. For I tell you that Christ has become a servant of the circumcised on behalf of the truth of God in order that he might confirm the promises given to the patriarchs, and in order that the Gentiles might glorify God for his mercy.

Paul's letter to the Romans, even though it has had a long and distinguished history and great impact on Christian theology throughout the centuries, is in the first instance a quite pastoral letter to a crisis situation in the Roman churches. He writes so that the rival factions—Jewish and non-Jewish Christians—might be unified and might follow Paul's example. In his letter opening, he writes of his desire to come to visit them: "For I am longing to see you so that I may share with you some spiritual gift to strengthen you—or rather so that we may be mutually encouraged by each other's faith, both yours and mine" (Rom. 1:11–12). In the same way, he wants to see these groups give and receive gifts, rejoicing together as fellow-citizens in the Kingdom of God.

5 EPHESIANS

This letter is likely the only one in Paul's letter collection that is not tied to any one situation. Paul spent more time with the Ephesian church than with any other. Though Antioch was his "home" church community, the 3 years he spent in Ephesus may be more than the entire time he spent in Antioch. The emotional farewell recorded in Acts 20 gives us a glimpse of Paul's attachment to the community in Ephesus. It is striking, therefore, to read the letter of Ephesians and find it so impersonal. There are no personal greetings in the letter, only the commendation of Tychicus, likely the letter's carrier (Eph. 6:21). These features, along with the fact that "in Ephesus" in Eph. 1:1 is missing from the earliest manuscripts, indicate that the letter was probably a circular letter sent around to churches in Asia Minor.

We might expect, then, that Ephesians would be Paul's most "theological" letter. After all, so the reasoning might go, if Paul is not addressing a specific situation and if he is indeed a theologian, then perhaps here we will witness him writing in theological terms. Some have outlined Ephesians along this line, calling chapters 1–3 "theology" and chapters 4–6 "ethics."

Such a conception is not entirely wrong, but it is a bit misleading. While passages such as Eph. 2:1–10 have functioned for many theologians as a key text in speaking of a "Pauline theology," there is so much more going on in this letter and we must understand the context within which this passage is situated. Paul, in this letter, speaks of the reality of the Kingdom of God and how communities of Jesus-followers ought to embody and inhabit that reality.

Ephesians begins like no other New Testament letter. It opens with a "berakah," a Jewish blessing formula that situates the letter in a worship setting. Paul speaks here of God's elective choice before time began and of God's plan for the gathering up of all things in Christ, "things in heaven and things on earth" (Eph. 1:10). While much of this material has been used for a doctrine of election, this is not at all Paul's intention. Paul's point here has to do with identity-formation. Much like discussions of election in the Scriptures of Israel, Paul aims to shape his readers' self-understanding and their imagination of God's work to redeem and remake the cosmos in Christ and through his people.

Paul then reports that he is praying to this end—that his readers might have the capacity to grasp the sort of divine power that is at their disposal (Eph. 1:15–19). A second prayer report appears in Eph. 3:14–19. In the rest of Ephesians 2–3, Paul narrates the triumph of God in Christ over Satan, the "ruler of the power of the air" (Eph. 2:2), and the powers and authorities that rule over the present evil age (Eph. 1:21). The whole of Ephesians 1–3, then, is really one large prayer report, with an elaboration of the kind of power that is available for the people of God—the kind of power that God used to defeat the powers of darkness. This power is demonstrated in God's freeing humanity from Satan's death-grip (Eph. 2:1–10) and in healing the deep ethnic divisions within humanity to create one new people among whom God now dwells by his Spirit (2:11–22).

Ephesians 4–6 is not exactly a section on "ethics," though this is not an entirely wrong description. In Eph. 4:17–24 Paul describes two realms within the cosmos and two ways of life that correspond to them. He speaks of the "old humanity" and the "new humanity," two realms that currently are up and running within the cosmos. Some Bible translations render these terms as the "old self" and the "new self," as if they were motivations within individuals. For Paul, however, these are two different groups within humanity and two different ways of life. The "old humanity" belongs to this present evil age which is doomed to destruction. It is that realm over which Satan rules, and which is corrupted by the fallen powers and authorities.

The "new humanity" is that realm that is made possible and sustained by the Spirit of God, and is made up of all who are "in Christ." This realm is the church, the arena over which Christ rules and which embodies the very life of Jesus presently on earth. Paul even calls the church the "body of Christ" (Eph. 5:30). The "ethic" that Paul advocates is one of transformation, whereby the church engages a dynamic of "putting away" practices of the "old humanity" and "clothes" itself with practices of the "new humanity" (Eph. 4:22–24). This is what Paul means when he speaks of being taught the truth as it is in Jesus (v. 21). What this entails more precisely is seen in 4:25–32 where he gives an exemplary series of practices to be left behind and renewed habits to be performed.

This letter, then, is again not a theological treatise as we might expect, but a narrative elaboration of how God has acted powerfully to call into being a new people—the church—and how that renewed people are to embody the reality of the Kingdom of God.

6 PHILIPPIANS

This is one of Paul's most personal letters, written to a church that was founded during his second journey and that he had visited during his third journey (Acts 20:3, 6). The Philippian church had sent

Paul a gift in care of Epaphroditus (Phil. 4:18), and Paul writes to thank them for their kindness. Paul also writes to calm their anxieties caused by their suffering on account of their conversion and his being imprisoned for his Christian ministry. He attempts to set them at ease by re-interpreting his imprisonment and their suffering from a heavenly perspective. Paul's imprisonment is no cause for alarm, since it is turning out for the spread of the gospel (Phil. 1:12–14) and is also resulting in Paul's salvation (Phil. 1:19). The NRSV translates the Greek word for "salvation" as "deliverance," as if Paul was saying that his imprisonment was turning out for his release from prison. Paul, however, means to say that his confidence and joy stems from his knowledge that God's way of bringing about his ultimate salvation is through this very sort of suffering.

Just as a renewed way of conceiving of Paul's imprisonment brings relief from anxiety, so too a new conception of the Philippians' suffering will bring comfort. Their maintaining confidence in the face of adversity is evidence of their ultimate salvation and of their opponents' ultimate destruction (Phil. 1:28).

The main "theological" contribution of this letter is the self-emptying passage in Phil. 2:5–11, but this appears in a context of exhortation and informs the entire letter. Paul does not aim to contribute to a doctrine of Christ ("Christology"), but is providing an example (the *ultimate* example!) for how the Philippians are to treat one another. In Phil. 2:2–4, Paul exhorts his readers to be unified, to do nothing from selfish ambition, and to pursue humility with regard to others. He counsels them to adopt the very same mindset as that of Jesus Christ in his self-expenditure. What follows is the single most formative passage for the development of Christology over the last two millennia:

[Christ Jesus], though he was in the form of God, did not regard equality with God as something to be exploited, but emptied himself, taking the form of a slave, being born in human likeness. And being found in human form, he humbled himself and became obedient to the point of death—even death on a cross. Therefore God also highly exalted him and gave him the name that is above every name, so that at the name of Jesus every knee should bend, in heaven and on earth and under the earth, and every tongue should confess that Jesus Christ is Lord, to the glory of God the Father. (Phil. 2:6–11)

This theologically rich passage, to make the point once more, appears in a context where Paul is shaping the imagination of his readers, turning them away from self-protection in a time of suffering, and toward self-expenditure. Just after this passage, Paul exhorts his readers to "work out your own salvation with fear and trembling," which amounts to a call to enter the narrative trajectory of Christ Jesus in order to share in the end of that narrative—salvation and exaltation. The pattern of self-expenditure unto death and exaltation shapes Paul's mention of Timothy and Epaphroditus in Phil. 2:19–30, and his autobiographical comments in Phil. 3:4–11.

Philippians is yet another instance of Paul reasoning theologically with a pastoral intention—to shape his readers' imaginations. Paul wants his readers to inhabit the life-giving Kingdom of God effectively, to demonstrate their citizenship by so doing, and to draw upon its resources for their own flourishing.

7 PHILEMON

Paul's letter to his friend, Philemon, garners perhaps the least attention. This may be because it does not contain much by way of "theology," having to do merely with a request that his friend be reconciled to the newly converted Onesimus. This letter perfectly exemplifies, however, Paul's vocation as herald of the Kingdom of God, re-shaping his readers' imagination regarding the reality and presence of God's reign in Christ and providing direction on how that reality is to be embodied in action.

In some way Paul had been responsible for the Christian conversion of Philemon (Phmn. 19), and knew of those that met as a Christian community in Philemon's home (Phmn. 1–2). At some point and through some unknown circumstances, Paul had encountered Onesimus and the latter had converted to Christian faith. It appears that Onesimus was Philemon's slave and was somehow indebted to him. It may be that Onesimus had run away from Philemon or that he has wronged him in some way and has fled for fear of punishment.

From his imprisonment, Paul writes to Philemon urging him to forgive Onesimus and to receive him back (Phmn. 17). Interestingly, and frustratingly for nineteenth-century British and American abolitionists looking for Scriptural support, Paul does not appeal for the release of Onesimus on the part of Philemon. We see Paul's vocation being fulfilled in the way he reasons with Philemon. The phrase that the NRSV translates as "the sharing of your faith" in Paul's prayer for Philemon in Phmn. 6, is better translated "the fellowship of your faith." It has to do with the reality that Philemon, Paul, and Onesimus all inhabit the Kingdom of God together. They are, therefore, intimately and vitally related to one another, being connected by God's Spirit in Christ. Paul prays that this reality "might become effective through the knowledge of every good thing which is in us unto Christ."

God is at work to shape those in Christ into communities that faithfully embody Jesus Christ on earth, and Paul bases his appeal to Philemon on this. The request that Paul makes of Philemon is consistent with citizenship in the Kingdom of God, and Philemon's fulfillment of it will be a demonstration of his faith in the reality and presence of the Kingdom of God. In this one-chapter letter from Paul to one of his friends, then, we see Paul's fulfillment of his vocation as a herald of the Kingdom of God, providing counsel and direction for how that reality might be embodied in a concrete situation.

8 CONCLUSION

This survey of Paul's letters demonstrates that he is not properly understood solely as a pastor, merely a missionary, nor only a theologian, especially in the contemporary senses of each of these terms. He does pastor churches, he goes on at least three missionary journeys in service of gospel proclamation, and, as we have noted, he writes to his churches casting theologically robust visions of the reality of the Kingdom of God as having invaded God's beautiful but broken creation. We have suggested that Paul is best regarded as a herald of the Kingdom of God, or, as he might put it, an apostle of the Lord Jesus Christ. He is utterly convinced that the crucified, risen, and exalted Jesus reigns as Lord over all creation and that the reign of God has been inaugurated among the followers of Jesus as the climax of the story of God redeeming the world. Paul writes in order to foster vibrant and fruitful communities that will embody this reality—communities that constitute the Kingdom of God on earth. Each of his letters—whether they appear more "pastoral" or more "theological"—serves this end at each and every point.

CHAPTER 3

THE STRUCTURE OF PAUL'S THOUGHT

We have already made the point in this book that Paul is not a theologian in the modern sense of that term, but that he does indeed theologize in that he addresses contingent and unforeseen church situations from a certain framework. As I hope to show, Paul's thought is most fundamentally shaped by the narrative of the Creator God and his call of Israel as his special possession. Paul regards the hopes of Israel and the promises given to the fathers as being fulfilled in Jesus Christ—in his being sent into the world by God, his death, resurrection, and ascension, and the sending of the Spirit. These climactic events have both radically altered reality and are most faithfully understood as completely in continuity with how God has always worked in the world with his people. In this chapter, then, we will rehearse this narrative and draw out several other essential features of Paul's thought.

1 THE NARRATIVE PAUL INHABITS

The God of Israel created the world and everything in it. Seizing control of a primeval condition of chaos and disorder, God spoke a creative word, ordering the world and placing humanity within the garden of Eden. God had designed the world as an arena for his joyful encounter with humanity—in the persons of Adam and Eve— and for the life-giving and fruitful engagement of Eve with Adam. God charged Adam and Eve to fill the entire earth and to cultivate it. They were to rule over creation in such a way that brought forth its fruitfulness. Further, they were to cultivate *shalom*, the flourishing of humanity and of creation together. In carrying out their commission to be stewards together over God's creation on God's behalf, they carried out their roles as *the image of God*.

God and humans have a cosmic enemy, it turns out, and this enemy is embodied in a serpent that tempts humanity to reject their proper role within creation as the "glory of God," another term Paul uses to speak of humanity in *the image of God*. Humanity was deceived "by the lie" and surrendered the role of being in the image of God, preferring idolatry (Rom. 1:23). This meant that humans no longer ruled over creation in the name of the one true God who created all things, and they no longer sought to cultivate *shalom*, looking after God's good world in harmony with others. Humanity now denies the truth that creation belongs to God and no longer lives for the praise and enjoyment of God. They now exploit the creation for short-term and selfish pleasures, seeking to dominate it and exploit fellow humans. Believing the lie of the serpent and seeking to take the place of God, humanity has set off on a course of self-destruction.

In response to this, God makes promises to redeem and reclaim his creation and to defeat his cosmic enemy. Interestingly, God promises to do this through humanity, the offspring of the woman (Gen. 3:15). God begins to fulfill these promises by calling Abraham, promising to make of his descendants a great nation and through it to redeem the world (Gen. 12:1–3). During a long sojourn in Egypt, in which they are enslaved and oppressed by the Egyptians, Israel grows into a large nation. God calls Moses to lead "his son," Israel, out of Egypt. The Egyptians resist the plan of God to redeem Israel from slavery and so the *exodus* becomes an opportunity for the God of Israel to display his strength in defeating Pharaoh and the gods of Egypt in cosmic battle. Looking ahead, the exodus from Egypt becomes the paradigm for how the prophets of Israel envision God's powerful work of salvation in the future. It also functions for Paul as the dominant image for God's salvation in Christ.

God's design in calling Israel out from Egypt is to make them a "holy nation," God's unique possession. Through Israel God aims to fulfill his promises to Abraham, making them a *blessing to the nations*. This is what is meant by Israel as a "Kingdom of priests." They were to represent God to the nations, and were to lead the nations in the worship of the one true God. This was to be their *holiness*—not that they were to be cut off from the nations, but that their national life was to be wholly different from the nations. They were to be a nation of justice and compassion, looking after the poor, the orphan, and the widow. There was to be no one needy among them, since they were all brothers and sisters, and the one true God whose world is one of plenty was to dwell among them uniquely. Further, they were to welcome the nations, developing relationships of mutual sharing in order to lead the nations in the way of the God of Israel, who was also the Great King over all the earth. If they carried out this risky mission, God would be their security and they would have no need of treaties.

As the story goes, however, Israel failed on a massive scale. Rather than being a *light to the nations*, they wanted to be *like the nations*, cultivating practices of injustice, exploiting the weak and defenseless, and adopting the worship of the gods of the nations. They could not trust God to protect them so they made treaties with the nations in order to guarantee their security. And they perverted God's Law delivered to them through Moses. They turned its practices into a set of distinctives that would cut them off from other nations, cultivating an arrogant and judgmental posture toward the nations. Rather than being agents of the life of God to the nations, they sought the destruction of the nations, imagining that God regarded outsiders with the same attitude of disgust.

God appealed to Israel through the prophets, but the nation persisted in resisting the redemptive call of their God. Refusing to be a light to the nations, Israel was sent into *exile* among the nations. God sent Israel into exile with a heavy and broken heart, however, and he promised that this was not the end of the story. He promised that he would send them an anointed one (a "messiah") through whom he would establish his Kingdom on earth once again. The nation would be brought back into the land from its exile and God would return once again to give life to his people. God would send his life-giving Spirit to breathe new life into dead bones and reconstitute Israel as a nation that would truly "know God." God would make them finally become the just nation that he called them to be. They would practice justice and look out for the poor, the orphan, and the widow, and they would lead the nations in the worship of the one true God.

In 458 BCE, a contingent of Israelites living in Babylon made a return to the land under the leadership of Ezra. While these Jews did eventually see the rebuilding of the temple, there was the tragic recognition that this was not the fulfillment of the promises. The temple they rebuilt was a pathetic imitation of the glorious Solomonic

temple that they had known years before. Subsequent Jewish generations also failed to see the arrival of the long-expected kingdom as
the land became little more than a sort of battleground of successive
imperial powers.

After the death of Alexander the Great in 325 BCE, the
land became a battleground between Alexander's successors, the
Seleucids, who ruled in Syria, and the Ptolemies, who ruled in
Egypt. Eventually, in 198 BCE the Seleucids gained control and in
175 BCE Antiochus IV, also called Antiochus Epiphanes, came to
power. He unleashed a devastating persecution against the Jews, and
his desecration of the temple provoked the rebellion begun in 167
BCE. The Maccabean revolt, begun by the Hasmonean priest
named Mattathias, and continued by his son Judas (nicknamed
"Maccabeus," which means "the hammerer") and his brothers, led
to the overthrow of the Seleucids and the eventual establishment, in
141 BCE, of Jewish self-rule until the arrival of the Roman general
Pompey in 63 BCE.

The Maccabean period is significant in that it shaped the imagination of Paul's (and Jesus') generation. They were waiting eagerly for
God's Messiah to come and deliver the nation from the oppression
of its enemies. When they imagined the one they were waiting for, it
was one like Judas Maccabeus—a violent warrior who would fight in
the name of Israel's God, wiping out the Romans and establishing
God's reign of justice and peace. As the years passed under the
Hasmoneans, however, the realization set in that just as the promises
had not been fulfilled with the return in the mid-fifth century BCE,
so now the Jewish rulers were compromised and corrupt.

As the first century dawned, the Jews, the inheritors of the story of
Israel and the people whose God was going to reclaim and redeem all
of creation, were waiting for God to fulfill his promises and to bring
salvation. And the salvation they envisioned, it should be noted, was
just as multifaceted as the rich promises given to Israel through the
prophets. Salvation included the forgiveness of sins, the return of the
presence of God among God's people, and the reconstitution of a
just people who would be the agents of God's mission to reclaim the
nations for the glory of his name.

This salvation, for Paul, came in the person of Jesus of Nazareth.
God had sent his Son Jesus as the long-promised "Messiah," God's
anointed agent through whom he would accomplish salvation. Things
had worked out much differently, however, than Paul would have

imagined before his conversion. He was waiting, along with most other Jews, for one like Judas Maccabeus, a violent revolutionary figure who would lead a movement to defeat the Romans and initiate God's reign and judgment of the nations.

Jesus was no Judas. He came preaching peace and forgiveness, calling followers who would take up their cross of self-expenditure and ministry for the sake of others. He gathered to himself a group of followers who were social outcasts who earned, together with Jesus, the disapproval of the leaders of the Jews. The Kingdom of God, according to Jesus, was not a reign of judgment and exclusion of those who do not measure up to culturally generated standards. It was, rather, one in which all were welcome regardless of credentials.

Jesus' ministry led to his rejection by Israel and ended in his death on a Roman cross. While this can only be interpreted as the utter and final defeat of God's purposes at the hands of a rebellious humanity, God overcame this ultimate injustice by raising Jesus from the dead and seating him on God's own cosmic throne. God also sent his Spirit—the Spirit of Jesus—to gather up his people, the church, and to dwell among them. The action of God in the death, resurrection, and exaltation of Jesus, and the sending of the Spirit, became the climactic events that determine everything for Paul and radiate significance and transformative power.

The narrative of the Creator God who aims to enjoy his creation along with his creatures and to see them flourishing in his redeemed and renewed creation finds its climax in the death, resurrection, and ascension of Jesus, along with the sending of the Spirit. This is the narrative framework that shapes Paul's vision of reality. Working from this fundamental narrative, we will draw out the significant factors that determine Paul's thought.

2 THE CROSSOVER OF THE AGES

Paul's understanding of his current location in the story of Israel's God and his work in the world is a transformation of his inherited narrative. He regards the present as the *crossover of the ages*. This notion will inform how it is that throughout Paul's letters he regards the singular "moment" of the death, resurrection, and ascension of Jesus Christ in two ways. First, that moment is the decisive day when judgment and salvation were accomplished, the long-expected moment of victory and divine triumph. In this sense, God has fulfilled his promises in Jesus and the sending of the Spirit. In another sense, however, God has confirmed in Jesus and the sending of the Spirit that his promises are going to be fulfilled in the future. The ultimate day of victory is still on its way. The death and resurrection of Jesus and the sent Spirit are *anticipatory* events, looking forward to God's climactic consummation of salvation and the judgment of God's enemies.

According to Jewish expectation, stemming from the Scriptures of Israel, the people of God were waiting for the "day of the Lord," the arrival of the climactic moment when God would save his people Israel, judge their enemies, and transform the entire creation. He was going to bring the present evil age to a close and bring in the age of the Kingdom, the new creation when all things would be made new and God's own presence would come to re-inhabit his good world. Such a vision of two distinct ages would look like this:

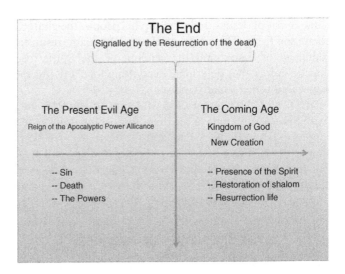

For Paul, the death and resurrection of Jesus becomes that long-awaited day of judgment, and the new age has indeed already arrived with the pouring out of the Spirit of God on God's people, now made up of Jew and gentile, people from every nation integrated into one new people. What is unique about Paul's thought, as we have noted above, is that while the "day of the Lord" has arrived, we still await the future "day of the Lord." Because of this, the new age has *already* arrived, but it is *not yet present in its fullness*. God has accomplished salvation decisively in the death and resurrection of Christ, but the full restoration of creation will only come in the future. The long-expected "day of the Lord," becomes for Paul the "day of Christ" (Phil. 1:6, 10), the future day of judgment and salvation. For Paul, therefore, salvation is "already," but "not yet," in that the work of God to restore creation has been *inaugurated* and will be *completed* at the future day of Christ.

Paul lives, therefore, and the church exists "between the times"; *after* the death and resurrection of Christ and the sending of the Spirit, but *before* the return of Christ to restore creation completely and to bring in the fullness of God's new creation—a new heavens and a new earth with Jesus Christ ruling as King on earth. The present situation according to Paul, a transformation of Jewish expectation, looks like this:

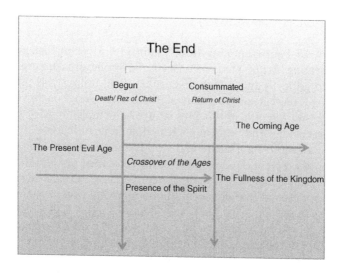

There are two ages up and running—the new age, begun by the death and resurrection of Jesus and the presence of the Spirit—and the old age, or the present evil age, which is still ruled by Satan, the "god of this age" (2 Cor. 4:4). At the cross, Jesus Christ delivered the fatal blow to Satan, fulfilling the promise God made to Adam and Eve that he would defeat his cosmic enemy through humanity (Gen. 3:15). When God raised Jesus from the dead, God initiated the destruction of this present evil age, and the task of Christ during the remainder of this age is to complete the destruction of his enemies. Paul elaborates on the relation of the resurrection of Jesus to his ultimate cosmic triumph in 1 Cor. 15:

> But in fact Christ has been raised from the dead, the first fruits of those who have died. For since death came through a human being, the resurrection of the dead has also come through a human being; for as all die in Adam, so all will be made alive in Christ. But each in his own order: Christ the first fruits, then at his coming those who belong to Christ. Then comes the end, when he hands over the kingdom to God the Father, after he has destroyed every ruler and every authority and power. For he must reign until he has put all his enemies under his feet. The last enemy to be destroyed is death. For God has put all things in subjection under his feet. (1 Cor. 15:20–27)

In v. 27 Paul is quoting from Psalm 110, a psalm that portrays God seating his anointed one on a cosmic throne and commissioning him to go forth and defeat his enemies. Paul utilizes this psalm to speak of the current situation of the exalted Jesus on his cosmic throne and his task in this present age to completely wipe out his cosmic enemies and bring in his Kingdom in its fullness.

According to Paul's inherited worldview, the resurrection of the dead was an event that happened at the end of the age and the dawn of the new creation. This would represent the ultimate defeat of death, the signal that death could no longer hold those whom God wanted to reclaim. That God raised Jesus from the dead as the "first fruits"—the first human to be raised from the dead—signaled the initiation of the new age of the Spirit and the inauguration of God's new creation. Again, however, it is not here in its fullness, since Paul still looks forward to the final destruction of death. We can say, then, that the present evil age is going down to destruction because of the fatal blow dealt by God, and the full realization of the new age awaits the future day of Christ.

This "already but not yet" dynamic is seen in a few other passages in the Corinthian correspondence. In 2 Cor. 1:20–22, Paul says this at the end of a discussion of his travel plans:

> For in [Jesus] every one of God's promises is a "Yes." For this reason it is through him that we say the "Amen," to the glory of God. But it is God who establishes us with you in Christ and has anointed us, by putting his seal on us and giving us his Spirit in our hearts as a first installment.

Paul here calls Jesus God's "yes" that his promises are going to be fulfilled in the future. Paul also refers to a "seal" that God has put on Paul and his readers, marking them in some way as his own special possession. This corresponds to the role of the Spirit, God's very presence among the Corinthian church, as a "first installment," a guarantee of the fullness of the Spirit that Paul and his readers will enjoy in the coming age. This "not yet" dimension is met by one of Paul's "already" statements in 1 Cor. 10:11, calling his readers those "on whom the ends of the ages have come."

This scenario, as we will see throughout the remainder of this book, has massive implications for every aspect of Paul's thought, including his discussions of the character of the church, the relationship of the church to the world, the nature of Christian existence, and the character of his own ministry.

3 AN APOCALYPTIC VISION OF REALITY

Paul envisions, in Christopher Rowland's phrase, "an open heaven."[1] The stage on which the drama of Scripture—and thus of all reality—unfolds is a cosmic stage. In ancient worldviews, just as in many cultures in the world today, the drama of everyday life included *suprahuman* actors—intelligent beings that inhabit the heavens and control the destinies of individuals and nations as well as the courses of peoples' daily lives. To understand Paul rightly, we must note that there are more actors on the cosmic stage than we typically imagine.

For Paul, Satan is a personal agent of evil in the world, the chief cosmic enemy of God seeking to dominate and despoil God's good world. Paul calls him the "god of this world" who blinds the minds of unbelievers "to keep them from seeing the light of the gospel of the glory of Christ" (2 Cor. 4:4). It seems that the manner in which Satan does this is through sowing corrupted ideologies and destructive patterns of life within creation, luring humanity to live in ways that are enslaving and oppressive. Satan is, after all, the "ruler of the power of the air," the realm of ideologies, cultural prejudices, and well-worn patterns of thought. In this role, he controls "the spirit that is now at work among those who are disobedient" (Eph. 2:2). Because of this, Paul is eager to help his churches develop discernment. He says to the Corinthians, "But I am afraid that as the serpent deceived Eve by its cunning, your thoughts will be led astray from a sincere and pure devotion to Christ" (2 Cor. 11:3).

In league with Satan are the powers and authorities, who appear to have been part of God's originally good creation, assigned to rule over aspects of creation and over the conduct of nations as God's stewards. They have rebelled in some way and now pervert their original commission by enslaving and dominating their appointed realms rather than overseeing them on behalf of the one true God. They do this, like the "god of this age," through corrupted and enslaving ideologies. Paul has these figures in mind in Col. 2:8 when he warns:

> See to it that no one takes you captive through philosophy and empty deceit, according to human tradition, according to the *elemental spirits of the universe*, and not according to Christ.

He uses the same Greek phrase to speak of these cosmic powers in Galatians 4, referring to his readers' condition before their conversion and reception of the Spirit. The Galatians were "enslaved to the elemental spirits of the world" (v. 3), but now have been redeemed and adopted as children (v. 5). "Why," he asks, "do you want to turn back again to the weak and beggarly elemental spirits? How can you want to be enslaved to them again"? (v. 9).

These powers were also responsible for the death of Jesus. In a discussion in which he contrasts the wisdom of God and the wisdom of the world, Paul says this:

> Yet among the mature we do speak wisdom, though it is not a wisdom of this age or of the rulers of this age, who are doomed to perish. But we speak God's wisdom, secret and hidden, which God decreed before the ages for our glory. None of the rulers of

this age understood this; for if they had, they would not have crucified the Lord of glory. (1 Cor. 2:6–8)

In Paul's inherited Jewish worldview, these cosmic rulers often stood just behind the scenes and influenced events to see to it that certain results were brought about. For Paul, these fallen cosmic rulers apparently knew that their scheme of grasping after God's world and holding it in their grip was threatened by the arrival of Jesus on the scene. They saw to it, therefore, that he was put to death, not realizing that according to God's upside-down wisdom that subverts all human pretensions and evil strategies, the death of Christ was also his victory, and their apparent victory was their own defeat.

Sin and Death are two more cosmic enemies. Sin, for Paul, is not merely something that humans do in violation of God's Law though it is that in some instances (e.g., Rom. 6:15). Sin is also a cosmic power that has had a hand in hijacking God's world, a parasite, a force that causes the self-destruction of humanity. We see this in Romans 6, where Sin has an ambition; to exercise dominion over the Roman congregations:

Therefore, do not let sin exercise dominion in your mortal bodies, to make you obey their passions. No longer present your members to sin as instruments of wickedness, but present yourselves to God as those who have been brought from death to life, and present your members to God as instruments of righteousness. For sin will have no dominion over you, since you are not under law but under grace. (Rom. 6:12–14)

Further, in Rom. 7:13, Sin schemes against Paul (or the entity or person to whom Paul gives voice) to work death in him:

Did what is good, then, bring death to me? By no means! It was sin, working death in me through what is good, in order that sin might be shown to be sin, and through the commandment might become sinful beyond measure.

The personification of Sin as an actor in the cosmic drama has precedent in the Scriptures of Israel. Genesis 4 depicts an interesting conversation between God and Cain. After he developed a jealousy toward Abel because the latter's sacrifice was deemed acceptable to

God, whereas his was not, Cain became very angry. God tells Cain, "If you do well, will you not be accepted? And if you do not do well, sin is lurking at the door; its desire is for you, but you must master it" (Gen. 4:7). Here, too, Sin has an intention, acting as a force in creation that seeks to enslave humans where they choose to plot evil and give in to anger, seeking the destruction of others.

Death, for Paul, is also an entity with a will. It is not just something that awaits the end of each person's life. Like Sin, Death can exercise dominion (Rom. 6:9). Death is also the ultimate enemy that Christ will defeat (1 Cor. 15:26), and he will do so by giving life to all those who follow him in faith, raising them from the dead. Death has been defeated by being transformed from an enslaver of humanity into a doorway to immortality. This leads Paul to exclaim that "Death has been swallowed up in victory. Where, O Death, is your victory? Where, O Death, is your sting?" (1 Cor. 15:54–55).

J. C. Beker has called this matrix of forces the "apocalyptic power alliance"; suprahuman powers that work to enslave humanity and oppress creation, preventing it from experiencing shalom according to the Creator God's design.[2] In the death and resurrection of Jesus, God struck the decisive blow to these forces, shaking loose their grip on creation and humanity, and signaling their ultimate defeat. Paul comments on this briefly in Col. 2:6: "Divesting himself of the rulers and authorities, he made a public display of them triumphing over them by the cross."

Much like the text in 1 Corinthians where Paul cites the powers' scheming to put Jesus to death, in this passage he portrays the powers as piling on him and making sure that he went down to death. Jesus, however, being raised by God from the dead, undoes death and turns it in on itself, reversing it and taking away its sting. He transforms death into a doorway. He then parades his defeated captives on a triumphant victory march on his way to his heavenly throne, where he now sits exalted "far above all rule and authority and power and dominion, and above every name that is named, not only in this age but also in the age to come" (Eph. 1:21).

During this present era, the crossover of the ages, these powers still exercise some sort of dominion and their influence is still significant. But they have been exposed and mortally wounded, and their power is diminished. The exalted Lord Christ is on a mission to completely destroy them during this age and he will finally do so at the end of the age—"the day of Christ." The church has access to the power of

God, because of the presence of the Spirit of God, in order to resist these powers and their evil schemes. In a familiar but striking passage, Paul exhorts his readers:

> Finally, be strong in the Lord and in the strength of his power. Put on the whole armour of God, so that you may be able to stand against the wiles of the devil. For our struggle is not against enemies of blood and flesh, but against the rulers, against the authorities, against the cosmic powers of this present darkness, against the spiritual forces of evil in the heavenly places. Therefore take up the whole armour of God, so that you may be able to withstand on that evil day, and having done everything, to stand firm. (Eph. 6:10–13)

Grasping this apocalyptic perspective on reality offers much help for understanding several passages in which Paul discusses the Mosaic Law. It is striking that in the two major epistles where Paul discusses the relationships between faith in Christ, the Mosaic Law, Judaism, and Jew-gentile relations, an apocalyptic perspective is brought to bear. In Paul's view, the apocalyptic power alliance hijacked God's good gift of the Law and used it to enslave Israel and humanity. This is precisely Paul's point in Romans 7:

> So the law is holy, and the commandment is holy and just and good. Did what is good, then, bring death to me? By no means! It was sin, working death in me through what is good, in order that sin might be shown to be sin, and through the commandment might become sinful beyond measure. For we know that the law is spiritual; but I am of the flesh, sold into slavery under sin. (vv. 12–14)

The Law remains God's good gift, but Sin and Death have conspired to hijack it and pervert it into a means of enslaving God's people, setting them against each other. The church has the capacity, however, to resist this dark scheme. They must read Scripture in accordance with the aims of the Spirit, rather than in accordance with the aims of Sin and Death (Rom. 8:2). The Spirit desires the unity of Jews and gentiles in the church, and reading Scripture to foster unity and faithfulness will bring life. Sin and Death, however, desire division and destruction, and reading Scripture to bolster any one group's claims to superiority will result in a fractured community.

4 SALVATION

Salvation, for Paul, has a variety of dimensions, and we have hinted at some of them already in the last few chapters. We have discussed the "already/not yet" aspect of salvation, how it is that the long-awaited day of salvation has already come, but that the people of God still await the future day of salvation. Paul also describes salvation using a variety of metaphors, so that we can imagine a many-sided diamond, appreciating the variegated beauties as we behold it from different perspectives. We will consider only a few crucial aspects and their significance.

4.1 Union with Christ

The fountainhead from which all the blessings of salvation flow, of course, is that God has united believers to Christ. Believers have been baptized into Christ (Rom. 6:3) so that Paul considers the entire church, made up of male and female believers of all races and ethnicities, as being "in Christ," a phrase he uses throughout his letters. Because they are united to Christ by the Spirit, believers have been crucified together with Christ (Gal. 2:20), they have been rescued out of the present evil age (Gal. 1:4), and have been transferred into the Kingdom of God's beloved Son (Col. 1:13). Because of this union with Christ, believers are reconciled to God. Their relationship to God is even more intensely intimate than this, actually, since by virtue of their union with Christ believers are drawn up into God himself. In Col. 3:3, Paul says that "your life is hidden in Christ in God."

4.2 The Spirit of God

This union with Christ and existence within God himself is brought about by God's Spirit. God had promised in the Scriptures of Israel that he would send his Spirit—God himself—to dwell among his people, giving them life, with the dawning of the new age. This new age has come *already* even though we await its fullness in the future, and it is effected and mediated by the Spirit. That is, the Spirit of God mediates the presence of God and the resurrection-powered realities of the coming new age to communities of God's people—to the church. In every place where Paul sees churches created, made up of those who respond to his gospel proclamation of the arrival of the

Kingdom, God himself is present by his Spirit. Paul asks the Corinthians, "Do you not know that you are God's temple and that God's Spirit dwells among you?" (1 Cor. 3:16).

God's Spirit not only unites believers to God but also unites believers to one another in "the body of Christ." In this sense, the exalted Lord Jesus is also fully present with church communities by the Spirit so that, as we will see, churches are to live out the life of Jesus himself on earth as the incarnate love of God. In Eph. 2:13–16, Paul discusses the union of formerly disparate groups in one new humanity, so that reconciliation is both, we might say, horizontal and vertical.

4.3 New creation

As we have already indicated, church communities are outbreaks of the new age, outposts of new creation existence where the power of the coming age is fully present. In this sense, Christian communities are instances of the Kingdom of God, a related expression also synonymous with being "in Christ" and "in the Spirit." In this sense, salvation is a place, a location on the cosmic map. Salvation involves being transferred from this present evil age into the Kingdom of God—into the realm of new creation where Christ is Lord and where the resurrection power of God operates because of the presence of the Spirit. Paul speaks of this reality when he says that:

> He has rescued us from the power of darkness and transferred us into the kingdom of his beloved Son, in whom we have redemption, the forgiveness of sins. (Col. 1:13)

Paul's exhortations to the Galatians come into sharp focus when we understand that he is speaking of these two realms up and running in reality. In his greeting, he speaks of "the Lord Jesus Christ, who gave himself for our sins to deliver us out of the present evil age" (Gal. 1:3–4). And in his closing, he says, "May I never boast of anything except the cross of our Lord Jesus Christ, by which the world has been crucified to me, and I to the world" (6:14). Paul has been brought from the present evil age into the realm of the Spirit, and his incorporation into the death and resurrection of Christ, by the Spirit, has brought about this transfer. This vision explains his words in Gal. 5:25: "If we live in the Spirit, let us conduct our lives by the Spirit."

We might depict these two cosmic realms as follows:

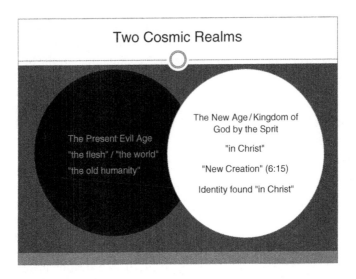

The ages overlap because, as we said above, we live in the crossover of the ages when both are up and running—the present evil age coming apart and headed for destruction, and the new age of the Spirit headed for its end in the eternal Kingdom of God. The church is to grow into its identity as God's new people, putting off practices characteristic of the present evil age.

4.4 TEMPORAL ASPECTS

Paul considers salvation from several temporal perspectives. There is an *initial* point when salvation arrives, or when people convert to Christ (1 Thess. 1:9–10; Eph. 1:12–13). Salvation is also an *ongoing* phenomenon, and Paul speaks of "those who are being saved" (1 Cor. 1:18). In this sense, salvation calls for ongoing participation on the part of believers. Paul speaks in several places of perseverance and of "continuing in the faith." In Col. 1:22–23, Paul says that God

has now reconciled in his fleshly body through death, so as to present you holy and blameless and irreproachable before him—provided that you continue securely established and steadfast in the faith, without shifting from the hope promised by the gospel that you heard.

God is also involved to sustain the participation of believers in new creation existence. Based on the Philippians' record of sharing in his gospel ministry, Paul is confident "that [God] who began a good work among you will bring it to completion by the day of Jesus Christ" (Phil. 1:6).

Finally, salvation involves the ultimate consummation of all things in the end. That salvation still lies in the future is apparent, not only from Paul's words in the Philippians text just quoted, but also from Rom. 13:11, where Paul says that "salvation is nearer to us now than when we became believers." The final moment of salvation will involve the resurrection of the dead in Christ and the transformation of creation into the fullness of the Kingdom of God.

There is much more to be said about the character of salvation, very obviously. We have not touched on the richness of the varied metaphors Paul employs, such as justification, reconciliation, redemption, and adoption as children, but because of limitations on space it must be sufficient to say that when Paul does call upon these metaphors he does so in order to speak of the salvation realities that we have just discussed.

5 THE IDENTITY AND MISSION OF THE CHURCH

We have already said much about the nature of the church and its identity as the new creation people of God, the Kingdom of God on earth where God dwells by his Spirit. We must also consider the church's identity through the mission of Israel as we have discussed it in the Scriptural narrative. Israel was called to be a "holy nation," a radically different people with an alternative mode of life. They were to look after the needy among them, caring for the poor, the orphan, and the widow. They were to cultivate and practice creational rhythms, working and resting after the Sabbatarian pattern God had set in his creation and rest from creation. And they were to be a light to the nations, a Kingdom of priests who would bring the life of God to the nations and call the nations to serve the one true God.

The identity and mission of the church, for Paul, is in direct continuity with the commission of Israel, which is why Paul refers to the Galatians as "the Israel of God" (Gal. 6:16). The church is to embody the life of God on earth by caring for the needy (cf. Gal. 2:10; 6:9–10; 2 Cor. 8:1–15), by being a community of reconciliation and peace-making, and by pursuing unity. The church also currently plays the role of light to the nations, witnessing to the wider culture of the life of God and the coming Kingdom (Phil. 2:15). This is not to say, however, that the church replaces Israel, or that Paul regards God as having rejected the Jews. On the contrary, Paul discerns that God is currently fulfilling Israel's mission of bringing the nations to himself before he then fulfills his promises to redeem Israel (Rom. 9–11).

The church, then, is not only to be the light to the nations but is itself the fruit of Israel's mission. In the Scriptural narrative, the nation had failed in its mission to be a light to the nations, but this role was picked up and re-performed successfully by Jesus, who became a light to the nations. In the death, resurrection, and ascension of Jesus and the sending of the Spirit, God is fulfilling the promises to Abraham and the gathered church—made up of Jews and gentiles ("the nations")—is becoming what Israel was to produce. The church is the fulfillment of the prophets' vision for Israel and the nations to gather together to worship the one true God, the God of Israel and the Father of Jesus (Eph. 2:20–22; Rom. 15:5–13).

The church is also the arena in which God displays his cosmic triumph over the powers that rule the present evil age. According to Paul's apocalyptic gospel, the Son of God was sent into God's enslaved creation—enemy territory—and triumphed through his death at the hands of the powers, what turned out to be their own defeat. This decisive blow in Jesus' death and resurrection is followed by God's establishment of new creation outposts throughout the world, signs to the powers of their defeat, the exaltation of the Lord Jesus, and their eventual destruction at the final day. In Eph. 3:10, Paul says that God's creation of the church through the preaching of the imprisoned Paul serves as an object lesson of God's wisdom to the cosmic rulers and authorities.

6 THE COMING JUDGMENT

For Paul's inherited Jewish worldview shaped by the Scriptural narrative, the future "day of the Lord" was the moment when the Creator God was going to vanquish his enemies, save his people, and completely restore and renew creation. On this day, the dead would be raised and join all humanity before the judgment of God. For Paul, this judgment in all its facets, has happened in an anticipatory sense at the death of Jesus, but will happen finally and publicly at what now is termed the "day of Christ."

This coming day provides motivation for Christian obedience. Paul tells the Corinthians that "we make it our aim to please [the Lord]. For all of us must appear before the judgment seat of Christ, so that each may receive recompense for what has been done in the body, whether good or evil" (2 Cor. 5:9–10). God will punish those "who do not obey the gospel of our Lord Jesus" (2 Thess. 1:8) and who have persecuted God's people (Phil. 1:28).

On this day God will raise the dead in Christ so that all in Christ will be transformed to fully participate in the reality of resurrection life (1 Cor. 15:51–54). Paul tells the Philippians that Jesus Christ "will transform the body of our humiliation so that it may be conformed to the body of his glory, by the power that also enables him to make all things subject to himself" (Phil. 3:21). The final salvation is also the moment when God will entirely transform creation so that it finally experiences freedom from its curse, under which it is groaning (Rom. 8:19–21). This day will come when the Lord Jesus is finished defeating his enemies, the final one being death itself. He will then establish his Kingdom and deliver it up to God so that the restoration of the creation—God dwelling in his temple, which is all of creation, along with humanity—will finally be realized.

7 DIVINE TRIUMPH

We must consider one final aspect of Paul's thought, and that is the *Theo*-centric orientation of Paul's consideration of all things. For about the last five hundred years, if not longer, students of Paul have read him as thinking about salvation with an anthropocentric orientation. That is, Paul has been read as if he is considering the benefits conferred upon humans in salvation, the order in which they are received, and the basis upon which they are possessed. Painting with a broad brush, we might say that this is one of the effects of the Enlightenment, which considered the human at the center of the universe.

This is not Paul's perspective. The central dramatic thread that holds together the Scriptural narrative is the account of the Creator God reclaiming his world by defeating the evil forces that have ravaged and marred its beauty. God has set out to vindicate his claim as the Great King over all the earth, the Most High God over all gods, the exalted one who alone gives life and breath and to whom everyone must give account.

This dramatic thread begins at creation, in which God brings order to a chaotic primordial state, and sets humanity within a beautiful garden. Outside of that garden is wilderness, but God intends to work together with humanity to spread his life-giving presence throughout creation. This project went off the rails fairly quickly in the biblical drama, of course, but it is never far from view. At the exodus, God displays his sovereign power over Pharaoh and Egypt, the mightiest nation of that time, in order to spread his fame. Throughout the psalms, God is depicted as holding back the forces of chaos to sustain his world, just as he holds back the raging nations in order to protect and sustain his people, Israel (Pss. 2:1–12; 46:1–3; 48:4–8; see also Job 38:8–11).

That the God of Israel was the Most High God, far more powerful than the gods of the nations was one of the central confessions of Israel's faith (Pss. 47:1–9; 96:4–5). Titles such as this, along with God's being the Great King over all the earth, reflected the conviction that the God of Israel was the only Creator God and that the gods of the nations were not really equal competitors, but creations of the God of Israel. They had been given authority to rule the nations but have rebelled and now enslave their nations in idolatry.

For Paul, God's action in Jesus and the Spirit have everything to do with God's triumph over all competing forces, especially the dark powers that enslaved his creation. In his death, Jesus struck the decisive blow to the powers, and this was vindicated when God raised him from the dead and seated him on his heavenly throne. Just as the God of Israel was "highly exalted above all gods" (Ps. 97:9), so Jesus is seated "far above all rule and authority and power and dominion, and above every name that is named, not only in this age but also in the age to come" (Eph. 1:21). In the sending of the Spirit, God called into being his new creation people in the midst of "enemy territory," confounding the powers with his wisdom (Eph. 3:10).

Even though it appears that the suffering of the church signals God's abandonment of his people or the strength of the powers of darkness and their ongoing domination of humanity, this is an illusion. God's triumph is seen in his overturning the schemes of darkness, utilizing the pressure of suffering to strengthen his own grip on his people. This is the logic that underlies Paul's words in Rom. 8:35–39:

> Who will separate us from the love of Christ? Will hardship, or distress, or persecution, or famine, or nakedness, or peril, or sword? As it is written, "For your sake we are being killed all day long; we are accounted as sheep to be slaughtered." No, in all these things we are more than conquerors through him who loved us. For I am convinced that neither death, nor life, nor angels, nor rulers, nor things present, nor things to come, nor powers, nor height, nor depth, nor anything else in all creation, will be able to separate us from the love of God in Christ Jesus our Lord.

The triumph of God in Christ is fundamental to the structure of Paul's thought, and though we have not discussed it in this chapter, this notion is reflected in Luke's account of Paul's preaching in the Book of Acts. For Paul, God is on a mission to reclaim his entire creation from the forces that have hijacked and perverted it. He is vindicating his role as Creator and his reign as sovereign King, and he will finally and publicly demonstrate his sovereignty and supremacy in his final triumph at the day of Christ. God aims to inhabit the whole world as his temple, dwelling among an entirely renewed humanity, made up of people from every nation. In subsequent chapters we will see how this structure informs Paul's conception of Christian existence and his own ministry, along with a number of more complicated discussions in his letters.

CHAPTER 4

THE CROSS AND THE SPIRIT: LIFE AS THE KINGDOM OF GOD

Paul does not, in any of his letters, lay out a comprehensive ethical vision. We have already made the point that Paul was not a theologian in the academic sense, elaborating a theological system in conversation with other professional theologians. Neither is he strictly an ethicist, setting out a moral code or an organized system of behavioral standards. We do not find in his letters that he is writing case law in the abstract, commenting on what to do if this or that situation should arise. As we have said, Paul writes to actual churches facing specific challenges or going through unique struggles, and he tailors his counsel to fit just those situations as he understands them. While he is not an ethical theorist, then, Paul does indeed have what we might call an *ethical vision*. He helps his churches to re-conceive and re-imagine their situations in light of Kingdom of God realities, and his counsel to them involves ethical reasoning to a high degree. Because of this, we can trace the basic contours of Paul's ethical vision and determine just how his thought "works" with regard to Christian conduct. When we do, we find that Paul's ethical vision is shaped by the death, resurrection, and ascension of Jesus, and the sending of the Spirit.

The pattern set by the death, resurrection, and ascension of Jesus is fundamental to Paul's thought and determines everything regarding the reality of the Kingdom of God. The life of the people of God is "cruciform"—which indicates existence in the shape of the cross. Not only this, but for Paul the creation of the church depends on the death, resurrection, and ascension of Jesus. The Spirit's work among the people of God is focused on producing in Kingdom communities this cruciform pattern of life. In this chapter, I will demonstrate how it is that the way of life that Paul envisions for his churches follows the pattern of the self-giving Jesus. We will look first at the cruciform life of Jesus and how this pattern is fundamental to his identity and to the character and identity of God. Then we will discuss how for Paul the death and resurrection of Jesus is the agency whereby God creates the church. This will be followed by a brief discussion of the ministry of the Spirit among the churches and the Spirit's aim of shaping Christian communities into the cruciform image of Jesus. Finally, we will see how these factors shape Paul's ethical vision, looking at how he patterns his own life after the cruciform life of Jesus and then how his ethical vision is shaped in a cruciform manner.

1 THE CRUCIFORM PATTERN OF JESUS

When Paul helps his communities solve their relational troubles or to imagine how to approach a challenge to their community life, his fundamental lens is the cruciform life of Jesus. We need to discuss this a bit further to understand just what we mean by this and how Paul utilizes this notion. This is seen perhaps most clearly in Philippians 2, where Paul anchors his exhortation to be unified in the self-expenditure and exaltation of Jesus.

In Phil. 2:1–4, Paul urges his readers to be unified in their participation in the new life created by the Spirit. He writes: "be of the same mind, having the same love, being in full accord and of one mind. Do nothing from selfish ambition or conceit, but in humility regard others as better than yourselves. Let each of you look not to your own interests, but to the interests of others." He bases this injunction on the behavior of Jesus Christ in 2:5–11:

> Let the same mind be in you that was in Christ Jesus, who, though he was in the form of God, did not regard equality with God as something to be exploited, but emptied himself, taking the form of a slave, being born in human likeness. And being found in human form, he humbled himself and became obedient to the point of death—even death on a cross. Therefore God also highly exalted him and gave him the name that is above every name, so that at the name of Jesus every knee should bend, in heaven and on earth and under the earth, and every tongue should confess that Jesus Christ is Lord, to the glory of God the Father.

Michael Gorman calls this passage "Paul's master story," the controlling narrative pattern that reveals the essential character of Jesus, through which Paul envisions his own ministry, the shape of Christian relationships, and the character of Christian community life.[1] I refer to this as a *"narrative* pattern" because it involves a sequence of events, each of which is indispensable. This narrative pattern stands in direct contrast to worldly modes of life, such as self-glorification, selfishness, fleshly indulgence, arrogance, pride, and other practices and attitudes that destroy relationships and communities. Several key elements make up this narrative pattern. First, Jesus possessed supreme status in his divine identity. He was God himself from all eternity and had rights to all the privileges that go along with this. Second, however, Jesus did not regard his divine identity as something to exploit for his own benefit. He did not utilize it as a lever to gain anything for himself, enhance his own comfort, or to preserve and protect his possessions.

Jesus, on the other hand, chose the route of complete self-expenditure and status renunciation. Rather than exploiting his position to improve his prospects, Jesus "emptied himself," humbling himself to take on humanity. Not only this, but Paul says in v. 8 that Jesus pursued a course of faithfulness to God's mission by giving himself unto death—the shameful death on a Roman cross. This downward trajectory—from divine status to humanity to shameful death—might be summed up in Gorman's succinct formula: "although [x], not [y], but [z]." That is, although Jesus existed as God [x], he did not exploit this [y], but rather chose the route of the cross [z].[2] This narrative pattern of self-emptying, renunciation of status, and death is called *cruciformity*.

This self-emptying, according to Paul, *is the reason God exalted him*. In v. 9, Paul says *"therefore* God highly exalted him," indicating that it was *because of* Jesus' downward trajectory, his self-emptying and his march to the cross—his cruciform, servant-shaped life—that God exalted him, giving him the very name of God himself—Yahweh. God's action in exalting Jesus to the highest place, the position in which he receives universal worship, and God's act of endorsing Jesus' trajectory by conferring on him God's own name, indicates that Jesus reveals the very character of the Creator God in his self-expenditure. As writers such as Gorman and Richard Bauckham have argued, Paul regards cruciformity to be the very character of God.[3]

This crucial connective—the "therefore" in v. 9—indicates that Jesus' cruciform pattern of life is *the singular pathway to exaltation*. In the remainder of Philippians, as we will see below, Paul makes exhortations based on this narrative pattern of self-emptying, renunciation of status, death, resurrection, and exaltation. Paul seeks to share in the sufferings of Christ in order to share in Christ's exaltation. The Philippians, too, are, to serve one another, adopting cruciform postures toward one another, so that they might share in the glory to be revealed at the day of Christ.

Paul's letters are filled with references to the self-expenditure of Jesus, as Paul works from this narrative trajectory to shape the community life of his churches. We will discuss a number of these passages below, but our point here is simply that the death of Jesus, along with his resurrection and ascension, determines Paul's ethical vision. Paul does not necessarily work from a set of principles to determine ethical exhortations. For Paul, this narrative is the fundamental thing—the sequence of events that reveals the cruciform character of God. Jesus, possessing privileges because of his divine identity, gave them up, refusing to exploit them for his own advantage. He became a servant and remained faithful to the point of being tortured and crucified on a Roman cross, the death of a political criminal. Because of his demonstrated faithfulness to God to the point of death, God raised him from the dead and exalted him to the place of cosmic lordship over all things. This is *cruciformity*—refusing to exploit advantages for selfish gain, taking the form of a servant—and it is the pattern of behavior that God rewards with exaltation and blessing. For Paul, this narrative trajectory, embodied by a community, is the manner in which the people of God enact the Kingdom of God.

2 THE CREATION OF THE KINGDOM

As we have seen, the death and resurrection of Jesus is fundamental for Paul in that it reveals the very character of God. Not only this, but the cruciform activity of Jesus is the means whereby God creates the church—the Kingdom of God. Just as the self-expending behavior of Jesus is subversive to worldly expectations, shaped as they are by self-seeking, selfishness, and greed, so the creation of the Kingdom is counter-intuitive. God does not initiate new creation through works of power or dominance, but through the (apparent) defeat and death of Jesus.

We have already spoken of the two realms Paul envisions within reality—the old age and the new age, also called the old humanity and the new humanity. Paul discusses the manner in which the new humanity is brought into existence in Eph. 2:13–16:

> But now in Christ Jesus you who once were far off have been brought near *by the blood of Christ*. For he is our peace; *in his flesh he has made both groups into one* and has broken down the dividing wall, that is, the hostility between us. He has abolished the law with its commandments and ordinances, *so that he might create in himself one new humanity* in place of the two, thus making peace, and *might reconcile both groups to God in one body through the cross*, thus putting to death that hostility through it.

The animosity that existed between Jews and gentiles in the old humanity has been eliminated by the death of Jesus. And it is the death of Jesus which brings into being this new humanity, made up of followers of Jesus from any and every ethnic, racial, and gender group. Because of their inclusion in the death of Jesus, believers have died to the old humanity, where racial, ethnic, and gender distinctions determined personal and social value. By virtue of their inclusion in the resurrection of Jesus, God brings both Jews and gentiles into the new humanity—the new creation space within reality, also called the Kingdom of God. In this space, everyone has a radically new identity and God has united everyone together as citizens of a new Kingdom, siblings in a new family where the primary identity of everyone is "follower of Jesus."

Paul reasons along similar lines in Col. 1:13–20. Believers have been transferred from the kingdom of darkness to the Kingdom of Jesus, a reality made possible by his death and resurrection. Believers' participation in the kingdom and the death and resurrection of Jesus appear here together:

> He has rescued us from the power of darkness and *transferred us into the kingdom of his beloved Son*, in whom we have redemption, the forgiveness of sins. He is the image of the invisible God, the firstborn of all creation; for in him all things in heaven and on earth were created, things visible and invisible, whether thrones or dominions or rulers or powers—all things have been created

through him and for him. He himself is before all things, and in him all things hold together. He is the head of the body, the church; he is the beginning, *the firstborn from the dead*, so that he might come to have first place in everything. For in him all the fullness of God was pleased to dwell, and through him God was pleased *to reconcile to himself all things*, whether on earth or in heaven, *by making peace through the blood of his cross.*

The participation of believers in this new age is brought about by the death and resurrection of Jesus. In Galatians 1, as we have seen already, Paul speaks of his own former participation in the old age, a form of existence in which his ethnic identity was of paramount importance. This was how Paul measured his own self-worth, and his value over-against others. Through his participation in the death and resurrection of Jesus, however, he has been brought out of the old age and delivered into the new age. Jesus Christ "gave himself for our sins to set us free from the present evil age" (Gal. 1:4). He refers to the cross of Christ in Gal. 6:14, "by which the world has been crucified to me, and I to the world." The death and resurrection of Christ brings about Paul's death to the old age and entrance into the new age—the new creation.

This same logic appears in 2 Cor. 5:14–17:

For the love of Christ urges us on, because we are convinced that one has died for all; therefore all have died. And he died for all, so that those who live might live no longer for themselves, but for him who died and was raised for them. From now on, therefore, we regard no one from a human point of view; even though we once knew Christ from a human point of view, we know him no longer in that way. So if anyone is in Christ – new creation! Everything old has passed away; see, everything has become new!

The death and resurrection of Christ are effective in bringing into existence the church, the Kingdom of God. This dynamic is effected by the Spirit, sent into the world to unleash God's resurrection and life-giving power. Because of Jesus' death and resurrection, existence in the new creation is based solely and only on participation in Christ, not one's ethnic identity nor any other social status.

3 THE SPIRIT AND CRUCIFORM COMMUNITIES

We have already indicated that for Paul church communities are dwelling places of God. The presence of the exalted Jesus dwells among churches, and this dynamic happens by God's Spirit. As Paul says in 1 Cor. 3:16, "Do you not know that you [as a corporate body] are God's temple and that God's Spirit dwells among you all?" In Ephesians 2, after announcing that God has made one new humanity out of various ethnic, racial, and gender groups, Paul utilizes the mixed metaphors of a building and a plant to speak of how God has built the church into a structure that is also organic, growing into a "holy temple in the Lord" (v. 21). Paul notes in the next verse that "in [the Lord] you also are being built up into a dwelling of God by the Spirit" (my translation). The Spirit of God is the animating force in the church, then, producing and sustaining Kingdom of God dynamics (cf. 1 Cor. 15:45; Gal. 5:25).

Paul envisions the aim of the Spirit of God as producing within Christian communities the radically cruciform love and subversive life of Jesus. He speaks of this mission of the Spirit in 2 Cor. 3:17–18:

> Now the Lord is the Spirit, and where the Spirit of the Lord is, there is freedom. And all of us, with unveiled faces, seeing the glory of the Lord as though reflected in a mirror, are being transformed into the same image from one degree of glory to another; for this comes from the Lord, the Spirit.

Being transformed by the Spirit into the image of the Lord means, of course, being shaped according to the same narrative pattern of cruciform love embodied and performed by Jesus while on earth. In Gal. 2:20–21, Paul speaks of the faithfulness of Jesus, and says that this faithfulness was expressed in his self-giving love. Later in this same letter, Paul speaks of the Spirit's work to produce these same practices in the life of the church:

> the fruit of the Spirit is love, joy, peace, patience, kindness, generosity, faithfulness, gentleness, and self-control. . . . And those who belong to Christ Jesus have crucified the flesh with its passions and lusts. If we live by the Spirit, let us also shape our conduct by the Spirit. Let us not become boastful, provoking one another, envying one another. (Gal. 5:22–26, my translation)

For Paul, then, churches are outposts of the Kingdom of God, communities where God's presence resides by the Spirit of Jesus. Because this is so, churches are the "body of Christ" on earth, embodying the self-giving love of God in the world, the same love for which Jesus set the pattern in his cruciform life. And the Spirit is shaping these communities accordingly, empowering them to embody the self-expending life of Jesus on earth.

4 DEATH AND RESURRECTION AS NORMATIVE ETHICAL PATTERN

This narrative pattern of self-expenditure—death, resurrection, and exaltation—becomes for Paul the normative pattern for Christian existence. Just as Jesus' own humiliation led to his exaltation, so too, participation in the self-emptying and suffering of Jesus produces exaltation with Jesus. This is the narrative pattern that God is effecting within communities of the Kingdom of God. According to Paul, participation in self-emptying and self-giving cements one's place in glory—guaranteeing participation in the resurrection unto life at the day of Christ. What is more, participation in the suffering of Jesus also draws upon and unleashes the resurrection power of God now. We see this both in Paul's ministry and in his ethical exhortations to his churches.

4.1 Paul's life and ministry

Paul's own life is shaped by the cruciform pattern of Jesus, which he clearly demonstrates in close connection with his master story in Phil. 2:5–11. Earlier in Philippians, Paul reveals his fundamental desire to have his life be an embodiment of the cruciform life and love of Jesus. He is resolved that "Christ will be exalted now as always in my body, whether by life or by death" (Phil. 1:20). Paul is in prison as he writes this letter, and it is likely that the Roman authorities signaled to Paul that if he commits suicide while incarcerated, they will spread the word to his followers that he died with honor. This was a common Roman tactic, which was, in some grisly sense, beneficial to the Romans and would possibly function as a best-case scenario to the incarcerated leader of a political movement. The Romans would be able to maintain peace and the leader of a movement could maintain his own honor and possibly leave his followers with some sense of satisfaction that their leader died honorably. The alternative—a torturous death—was not an attractive one. It was far more important, on a Roman view of things, to maintain one's own honor than one's life.

Paul likely was faced with this choice, and he provides a window for the Philippians into his own reasoning:

> For to me *to live* is Christ and *to die* is gain. But if I live on in the flesh, this is fruitful labor for me, and I do not know which to choose. And I am hard-pressed between the two options, having the strong desire to depart and be with Christ, for that is far better. But to remain in the flesh is more necessary for your sake. And convinced of this I know that I will remain and continue with all of you for your progress and joy in faithfulness. (Phil. 1:21–25)

Paul is faced with a choice. On one hand, he can choose his own gain, which takes the form here of accepting the Roman offer, losing his life and going to be with Christ. On the other hand, Paul can choose to go on living, which will mean continued suffering in prison and further discomfort and pain. He does not seem to have a guarantee that he will be released, but even if he is set free, his commission inevitably involves him in a life of pain and suffering. To go on living is the route of self-expenditure for the sake of the Philippian church, and this is the option Paul chooses. He will spend himself on behalf of others—the choice that exalts Christ, embodying the self-giving love of Jesus. To go on living—to refuse the Roman offer to take his own life and die with honor on their terms—is the "Christ" option, the choice that most accords with the cruciform pattern embodied by Jesus in 2:5–11.

The same pattern informs Paul's discussion of his past privileges in Phil. 3:4–11. He warns his readers to watch out for those who put confidence in the flesh, by which Paul means those who boast about their credentials, social status, or faithfulness to socially constructed standards. In terms of his Jewish heritage, Paul had every reason to boast (vv. 5–6), but he has come to regard these impressive credentials very differently now that his pursuit is to conform to the cruciform pattern set by Christ. His aim is to "know Christ and the power of his resurrection and the sharing of his sufferings by becoming like him in his death, if somehow I may attain the resurrection from the dead" (vv. 10–11). Faithful embodiment of the cruciform character of Jesus draws upon and releases the resurrection power of God now and secures one's place at the resurrection of the dead at the day of Christ in the future. Because of this, Paul happily suffers the loss of all credentials and privileges in order that he may "gain Christ" (v. 8)—in order that Paul might faithfully participate in the self-expending trajectory of Jesus.

Paul's cruciform ministry style is seen perhaps most clearly in his Corinthian letters. This may be the case because of the extreme cultural narcissism and preoccupation with image and performance that seems to have dominated Corinthian culture. Paul reminds his readers of his counter-cultural manner while he was among them:

> When I came to you, brothers and sisters, I did not come proclaiming the mystery of God to you in lofty words or wisdom. For I decided to know nothing among you except *Jesus Christ, and him crucified.* And I came to you in weakness and in fear and in much trembling. My speech and my proclamation were not with plausible words of wisdom, but with a demonstration of the Spirit and of power, so that your faith might rest not on human wisdom but on the power of God. (1 Cor. 2:1–5)

Paul envisions his presence in Corinth as a performance of the crucified Jesus and this was embodied by a ministry style of weakness. Paul consciously chose to avoid playing to the desires of the Corinthians for impressive speech and powerful rhetorical displays. This would have *obscured* the power of God. The eyes of faith see the subversive and unexpected power of God in the cruciform life of Jesus—his life of self-expenditure that subverts the Roman love of power and the Greek love of rhetorical displays and glorification of self.

He continues this discussion of his cruciform ministry in 2 Corinthians. He and his partners "do not proclaim ourselves; we proclaim Jesus Christ as Lord and ourselves as your slaves for Jesus' sake" (2 Cor. 4:5). Further, in a beautifully poetic passage, he describes how the treasure of the gospel proclamation is contained in pots designed for human refuse:

> But we have this treasure in clay jars, so that it may be made clear that this extraordinary power belongs to God and does not come

from us. We are afflicted in every way, but not crushed; perplexed, but not driven to despair; persecuted, but not forsaken; struck down, but not destroyed; always carrying in the body the death of Jesus, so that the life of Jesus may also be made visible in our bodies. For while we live, we are always being given up to death for Jesus' sake, so that the life of Jesus may be made visible in our mortal flesh. So death is at work in us, but life in you. (2 Cor. 4:7–12)

Paul envisions his ministry as one in which he embodies the death of Jesus, never seeking his own glory or to benefit from carrying out his commission as an apostle. Because he does this, God also works to manifest in Paul the life of Jesus. Paul's cruciform ministry, then, releases the resurrection power of God, which also effects life among the Corinthians. Paul's self-expending ministry, then, releases the resurrection power of God in both Paul and those to whom he ministers. Not only this, however, but participation in the self-expending life of Jesus now, which involves suffering and servant-hood, works to guarantee participation in the future resurrection and the eternal life and glory of God. This is the dynamic Paul refers to again in the paragraph that follows in 2 Corinthians:

But just as we have the same spirit of faith that is in accordance with scripture—"I believed, and so I spoke"—we also believe, and so we speak, because we know that the one who raised the Lord Jesus will raise us also with Jesus, and will bring us with you into his presence. Yes, everything is for your sake, so that grace, as it extends to more and more people, may increase thanksgiving, to the glory of God. So we do not lose heart. Even though our outer man is wasting away, our inner man is being renewed day by day. For this slight momentary affliction is preparing us for an eternal weight of glory beyond all measure, because we look not at what can be seen but at what cannot be seen; for what can be seen is temporary, but what cannot be seen is eternal. (2 Cor. 4:13–18)

Paul speaks again of his participation in the sufferings of Christ in his letter to the Colossian church. Paul says that he rejoices "in my sufferings for your sake, and in my flesh I am completing what is lacking in Christ's afflictions for the sake of his body, that is, the church" (Col. 1:24). This likely refers to Paul's apostolic ministry, which he envisions as an embodied performance of the very ministry of Jesus on earth. Just as Jesus gave himself unto death for the life of his people, so Paul fully gives himself to the suffering entailed in his ministry so that the church may receive the grace of Christ.

We have only mentioned a handful of passages that illustrate that throughout his letters Paul depicts his apostolic ministry as shaped by the death and resurrection of Jesus. He purposefully crafts his ministry to mimic the self-expenditure of Jesus. Paul embodies weakness to display fully the cruciform character of God in Jesus, knowing that the power of God is thereby unleashed. Further, Paul is confident that his own self-giving secures his participation in the resurrection to come.

4.2 Paul's exhortations

The cruciform character of Jesus is also the primary lens through which Paul envisions his counsel to his churches. In Philippians, Paul's rehearsal of the cruciform pattern of Jesus is preceded by his exhortation for the Philippians to be united and to "do nothing from selfish ambition or conceit, but in humility regard others as better than yourselves. Let each of you look not to your own interests, but to the interests of others" (Phil. 2:3–4). Further, after drawing out his own embodiment of cruciformity, Paul urges his readers to "join in imitating me, and observe those who live according to the example you have in us" (Phil. 3:17). To do otherwise is to "live as enemies of the cross of Christ" (v. 18), by which Paul means those who serve their own appetites and whose "minds are set on earthly things" (v. 19). Paul again brings to mind the resurrection hope involved in cruciform existence in vv. 20–21:

> But our citizenship is in heaven, and it is from there that we are expecting a Savior, the Lord Jesus Christ. He will transform the body of our humiliation so that it may be conformed to the body of his glory, by the power that also enables him to make all things subject to himself.

The end of a self-seeking life is destruction, while the end of a cruciform life is resurrection and transformation of the humiliated body into a body of glory at the day of Christ. Just as the humiliation of

Jesus led to exaltation and glorification, so believers' humiliation for the sake of Christ will result in exaltation and glory.

This very same vision shapes Paul's counsel to the Roman churches. As we discussed in Chapter 2, Paul writes to the Romans who are in the midst of a struggle over how to embody their identity as the people of God. Should they take on a gentile form of life, to the exclusion of Jewish Christians, or is it acceptable for the Jews to marginalize gentiles? Paul claims that their seeking to situate themselves over-against one another is sinful and destructive. They are reading Scripture wrongly, inadvertently subjecting themselves to the schemes of Sin and Death, cosmic figures that are seeking to destroy the Kingdom of God in Rome. These figures thrive when groups set themselves over-against each other, and in Rome the various groups' self-assertion is playing into the strategies of these evil figures.

The church must read Scripture according to the Spirit, in line with what God has done and is doing to unite Jew and gentile *in one new humanity*. This reading of Scripture and the community that results from it, will be cruciform, with various groups serving and loving each other, refusing to exploit any advantages for their own gain. This is what Paul means in Rom. 8:2, when he says that "the law of the Spirit of life in Christ Jesus has set you free from the law of sin and of death." Sin and Death seek to hijack the Law and use it for their evil purposes in the Kingdom of God. This is seen when groups cite Scripture to support their own claims to superiority over others. On the other hand, reading Scripture to develop cruciform community life resists these dark and destructive strategies. That is, a community that reads Scripture to inform servant-shaped lives and patterns of conduct becomes powerful against the aims of Sin and Death. This is, after all, the aim of the Spirit in the Roman community—to unite disparate and heretofore separated groups into one new humanity that embodies the life and love of Jesus.

Paul then reveals that the true identity of the people of God are those who suffer with Christ, whether Jew or gentile, male or female. The children of God are not those who are physically descended from Abraham (Rom. 4:16) nor those who conform to Jewish identity through prescribed practices. None of these criteria guarantee glorification with Christ on the day of Christ. Only those who suffer with Christ, irrespective of other group memberships, will be glorified with Christ.

If the Spirit of him who raised Jesus from the dead dwells in you, he who raised Christ from the dead will give life to your mortal bodies also through his Spirit that dwells in you. So then, brothers and sisters, we are debtors, not to the flesh, to live according to the flesh— for if you live according to the flesh, you will die; but if by the Spirit you put to death the deeds of the body, you will live. For *all who are led by the Spirit of God are children of God*. For you did not receive a spirit of slavery to fall back into fear, but you have received a spirit of adoption. When we cry, "Abba! Father!" it is that very Spirit bearing witness with our spirit that we are children of God, and if children, then heirs, heirs of God and joint heirs with Christ—*if, in fact, we suffer with him so that we may also be glorified with him.* (Rom. 8:11–17)

Both groups in the Roman fellowships are to love and serve one another, imitating the cruciform character of Jesus. At the climax of the letter, in Romans 15, Paul directly links the expectations of both groups and the conduct of Jesus Christ.

We who are strong ought to put up with the failings of the weak, and not to please ourselves. Each of us must please our neighbor for the good purpose of building up the neighbor. For Christ did not please himself; but, as it is written, "The insults of those who insult you have fallen on me." For whatever was written in former days was written for our instruction, so that by steadfastness and by the encouragement of the scriptures we might have hope. May the God of steadfastness and encouragement grant you to live in harmony with one another, in accordance with Christ Jesus, so that together you may with one voice glorify the God and Father of our Lord Jesus Christ. Welcome one another, therefore, just as Christ has welcomed you, for the glory of God. For I tell you that Christ has become a servant of the circumcised on behalf of the truth of God in order that he might confirm the promises given to the patriarchs, and in order that the Gentiles might glorify God for his mercy. (Rom. 15:1–9)

Rather than self-seeking, each group is to love and serve the other, and if this means the receipt of insults and slights, then this provides an opportunity to participate in the sufferings of Christ. Just as Jesus welcomed sinners from among both groups—Jew and gentile—so, too, these two groups are to welcome one another and participate with one another in giving glory to God.

Paul's exhortations shaped by cruciformity fill the Corinthian letters because the specific problem he perceives in the church is self-assertion and selfishness. In his opening he cites the development of factions and the quarrelsome character of their corporate life:

> Now I appeal to you, brothers and sisters, by the name of our Lord Jesus Christ, that all of you should be in agreement and that there should be no divisions among you, but that you should be united in the same mind and the same purpose. For it has been reported to me by Chloe's people that there are quarrels among you, my brothers and sisters. (1 Cor. 1:10–11)

In 1 Cor. 6:1–8, Paul condemns the practice of taking a fellow Christian to court. Paul maintains that disputes ought to be resolved and reconciliation achieved in the church. After all, he says, Christians will one day judge the world (v. 2). That Christians are taking their grievances against one another before non-Christian judges is a defeat for the church (v. 7). This is so because it is a sur-render of the very character of what it means to be the church. Such behaviors constitute a refusal to embody the Kingdom of God on earth, which operates in power when people choose self-expenditure over self-assertion. Paul claims that it is better to be wronged than to bring a case before the courts, since the absorption of a wrong pro-vides the opportunity to embody Kingdom practices of forgiveness and reconciliation. And if this leads to some sort of personal loss, then this is a fulfillment of a fundamental part of Christian identi-ty—to suffer loss for the sake of Christ, which works to guarantee a share in the resurrection at the day of Christ.

In 1 Cor. 11:17–34 Paul applies cruciform logic to the Lord's Supper. The concluding command in this passage is in v. 33: "So then, my brothers and sisters, when you come together to eat, wait for one another." Paul's exhortation has to do with behavior that follows the cruciform pattern set by Jesus. The wealthier Corinthians must refuse to exploit their advantages over others, but choose to use their resources to serve those who are in need. To behave selfishly in the church gathering by keeping the good food and wine only for those with higher social status is to incur the judgment of God (v. 29). It is a failure to participate faithfully in the Kingdom of God, and Paul indicates that when they do this, they ought not to call themselves the church nor call the meal the Lord's Supper. Conducting the fellowship meal in such a way that everyone waits for one another, making sure that everyone is served and included, on the other hand, is to "proclaim the Lord's death until he comes" (v. 26). The Kingdom of God is embodied through cruciform community practices of love and inclusion. Where there is exploitation of the weak and the presence of hierarchies based on social status, Paul discerns only the prospect of God's judgment.

In Eph. 4:25–5:2, Paul draws out the process of transformation whereby the church is to embody the life and love of Jesus. To enact the truth as it is in Jesus (v. 21), Paul instructs churches to be constantly eliminating practices that are characteristic of the old humanity (v. 22), to be renewed in their thinking (v. 23), and to cultivate practices that embody the new humanity that God has brought into being (v. 24). What follows is a paragraph filled with examples of how this might look (vv. 25–32). Each of the practices that must be put off are ones that embody selfishness, self-assertion, and exploitation of others. Those that must be developed are embodiments of cruciform community life, calling for self-expenditure and service to others. Paul sums up this paragraph in 5:1–2 by making explicit reference to the manner in which the Kingdom of God enacts and performs the cruciform pattern of Jesus: "Therefore be imitators of God, as beloved children, and live in love, as Christ loved us and gave himself up for us, a fragrant offering and sacrifice to God."

Paul makes explicit reference to the church's participation in the death and resurrection of Jesus in his exhortations to the Colossians in Col. 2:20–3:4. They ought not to give in to pressure and engage in harsh treatment of the body as an embodiment of Christian identity. Paul calls these sorts of practices "self-imposed piety" that are "of no value in checking self-indulgence" (2:23). Paul lays out an alternative vision:

> So *if you have been raised with Christ*, seek the things that are above, where Christ is, seated at the right hand of God. Set your minds on things that are above, not on things that are on earth, *for you have died*, and your life is hidden with Christ in God. When Christ who is your life is revealed, then you also will be revealed with him in glory. (Col. 3:1–4)

Paul here counsels the church on how to embody their current identity as those who belong to the age to come, no longer to this present evil age—a reality brought about by the death and resurrection of Jesus. And because their life is bound up in Christ, by virtue of their participation in the Kingdom of God, when Jesus Christ is publicly revealed at the day of Christ, they too will fully share in that glory (v. 4). Again, participation in the cruciform pattern of Jesus in the present brings about participation in glory at the future day of Christ.

5 CONCLUSION

Paul has much more to say, obviously, about how Christian communities are to embody their identity as the Kingdom of God, and Paul does address many more particulars than we have mentioned here. Our point, however, is simply that the primary lens for Paul's vision of Christian community life is the cruciform life of Jesus—his self-expenditure, his love expressed in his self-giving, his death, and resurrection. For Paul, God has endorsed this cruciform pattern of life in raising Jesus from the dead and conferring on him God's own name, demonstrating that God's own character is cruciform. These decisive acts of Jesus were powerful to create the church, God's new humanity, among which God dwells by the Spirit. And the Spirit is working among the people of God to conform them into God's own character so that the cruciform life of Jesus will be embodied by churches throughout the world.

CHAPTER 5

PAUL AND JUDAISM

Perhaps the thorniest and most contested current issue involved in Pauline studies today is his relationship to the Judaism in which he was nurtured. As we have already seen, Paul is a convert to "the Way," the Jesus movement. According to Luke's account in Acts, in which Paul several times recounts his version of things, this "conversion" involved a turn away from persecuting the church of Jesus Christ, and a commission to proclaim salvation to the gentiles. Further, in several of his most well-known letters (Galatians, Romans, and Philippians), Paul has extended discussions of his former life in Judaism, the Jewish people, Israel, and the gospel of Jesus. Paul appears to set Judaism over-against faith in Jesus Christ. He contrasts "works" and "works of Law" with "faith in Christ," in several pivotal passages. What does Paul mean when he sets these two in contrast? That Paul contrasts the gospel he preaches with Judaism in some sense is clear. The nature of this contrast, however, is the singularly most contested issue in Pauline studies over the last several decades, and is anything but clear!

In this chapter, I will introduce two available options for describing Paul's gospel as it relates to Judaism, or at least the Jewish convictions that Paul appears to critique. Scholarly opinions vary widely on this issue, but it is fair to say that two broad visions of Paul's critique have emerged. In an attempt to answer these questions, we will discuss what has come to be known as "the new perspective on Paul," along with what might be called a more "traditional perspective."

Before we rehearse these two broad interpretive perspectives, it will be helpful to see the main passages that are involved in the debate. In Gal. 1:13–17, Paul contrasts his advancement in Judaism with his obedience to the revelation of Jesus Christ by God.

You have heard, no doubt, of my earlier life in Judaism. I was violently persecuting the church of God and was trying to destroy it. I advanced in Judaism beyond many among my people of the same age, for I was far more zealous for the traditions of my ancestors. But when God, who had set me apart before I was born and called me through his grace, was pleased to reveal his Son to me, so that I might proclaim him among the Gentiles, I did not confer with any human being, nor did I go up to Jerusalem to those who were already apostles before me, but I went away at once into Arabia, and afterwards I returned to Damascus.

In Gal. 2:15–21, Paul draws a sharp contrast between two ways of seeking to be justified. On one side is "works of Law," "doing the works of the Law," and justification "through the Law." On the other is "faith in Jesus Christ," "faith in Christ," and being "justified in Christ."

We ourselves are Jews by birth and not Gentile sinners; yet we know that a person is justified not by the works of the law but through faith in Jesus Christ. And we have come to believe in Christ Jesus, so that we might be justified by faith in Christ, and not by doing the works of the law, because no one will be justified by the works of the law. But if, in our effort to be justified in Christ, we ourselves have been found to be sinners, is Christ then a servant of sin? Certainly not! But if I build up again the very things that I once tore down, then I demonstrate that I am a transgressor. For through the law I died to the law, so that I might live to God. I have been crucified with Christ; and it is no longer I who live, but it is Christ who lives in me. And the life I now live in the flesh I live by faith in the Son of God, who loved me and gave himself for me. I do not nullify the grace of God; for if justification comes through the law, then Christ died for nothing.

Perhaps the most difficult text in Galatians is 3:10–14. This is a very dense passage, regarded as one of the two or three most difficult in all of Paul's letters.

For all who rely on the works of the law are under a curse; for it is written, "Cursed is everyone who does not observe and obey all the things written in the book of the law." Now it is evident that no one is justified before God by the law; for "The one who is righteous will live by faith." But the law does not rest on faith; on the contrary, "Whoever does the works of the law will live by them." Christ redeemed us from the curse of the law by becoming a curse for us—for it is written, "Cursed is everyone who hangs on a tree"—in order that in Christ Jesus the blessing of Abraham might come to the Gentiles, so that we might receive the promise of the Spirit through faith.

Paul's letter to the Romans contains a number of similar passages that contrast "faith in Christ" with "Law" or "works of Law." A significant text is Rom. 3:21–31, which we will discuss at length below:

But now, irrespective of law, the righteousness of God has been disclosed, and is attested by the law and the prophets, the righteousness of God through faith in Jesus Christ for all who believe. For there is no distinction, since all have sinned and fall short of the glory of God; they are now justified by his grace as a gift, through the redemption that is in Christ Jesus, whom God put forward as a sacrifice of atonement by his blood, effective through faith. He did this to show his righteousness, because in his divine forbearance he had passed over the sins previously committed; it was to prove at the present time that he himself is righteous and that he justifies the one who has faith in Jesus. Then what becomes of boasting? It is excluded. By what law? By that of works? No, but by the law of faith. For we hold that a person is justified by faith apart from works prescribed by the law. Or is God the God of Jews only? Is he not the God of Gentiles also? Yes, of Gentiles also, since God is one; and he will justify the circumcised on the ground of faith and the uncircumcised through that same faith. Do we then overthrow the law by this faith? By no means! On the contrary, we uphold the law.

Paul changes up his language just a bit to articulate the contrast in Rom. 9:30–10:4. On one side, he speaks of "righteousness that is based on the Law," righteousness "based on works," "their own" righteousness. Israel, in following this pursuit, does so out of a "zeal for God" that is "not enlightened." On the other side is "righteousness through faith," righteousness that is gained "on the basis of faith," all of which is done by submitting to "God's righteousness."

What then are we to say? Gentiles, who did not strive for righteousness, have attained it, that is, righteousness through faith; but Israel, who did strive for the righteousness that is based on the law, did not succeed in fulfilling that law. Why not? Because they did not strive for it on the basis of faith, but as if it were based on works. They have stumbled over the stumbling-stone, as it is written, "See, I am laying in Zion a stone that will make people stumble, a rock that will make them fall, and whoever believes in him will not be put to shame." Brothers and sisters, my heart's desire and prayer to God for them is that they may be saved. I can testify that they have a zeal for God, but it is not enlightened. For, being ignorant of the righteousness that comes from God, and seeking to establish their own, they have not submitted to God's righteousness. For Christ is the end of the law so that there may be righteousness for everyone who believes.

One final text to consider along this line is Phil. 3:3–11, which draws the same contrast between a righteousness that comes through "faith in Christ" and "a righteousness of my own that comes from the Law."

For it is we who are the circumcision, who worship in the Spirit of God and boast in Christ Jesus and have no confidence in the flesh—even though I, too, have reason for confidence in the flesh. If anyone else has reason to be confident in the flesh, I have more: circumcised on the eighth day, a member of the people of Israel, of the tribe of Benjamin, a Hebrew born of Hebrews; as to the law, a Pharisee; as to zeal, a persecutor of the church; as to righteousness under the law, blameless. Yet whatever gains I had, these I have come to regard as loss because of Christ. More than that, I regard everything as loss because of the surpassing value of knowing Christ Jesus my Lord. For his sake I have suffered the loss of all things, and I regard them as rubbish, in order that I may gain Christ and be found in him, not having a righteousness of my own that comes from the law, but one that comes through faith in Christ, the righteousness from God based on faith. I want to know Christ and the power of his resurrection and the sharing of his sufferings by becoming like him in his death, if somehow I may attain the resurrection from the dead.

The contrast, then, is clear. Paul sees "faith in Christ," and the righteousness that comes through "faith in Christ" as in distinct contrast to a "righteousness that comes through the Law," "Law," and "works of Law." Why does Paul draw this contrast and what is the difference between these two dynamics? These questions get to the heart of Paul's gospel and his relationship to his Jewish heritage.

1 THE "TRADITIONAL PERSPECTIVE" ON PAUL

Stemming from Augustine (354–430 CE) and certainly since the Reformation (sixteenth century), a certain reading of Paul dominated. What we might call the "traditional perspective" on Paul and the Law entailed a very sharp contrast between Paul's gospel and his Jewish heritage. In drawing this sharp contrast between "faith in Christ" and "Law," Paul was opposing Jewish *legalism*. That is, what Paul rejected about Judaism is that it was a legalistic religious system. We can define legalism as seeking to accumulate merit through doing good deeds with the goal of presenting a claim to God for salvation. When Paul critiques "Law," "works of the Law," and "works," he is opposing an implicit Jewish legalism; the assumption that one's status before God is earned through merit gained through good deeds. Alternatively, Paul is commending "faith in Christ," understood as simple trust or belief in Jesus Christ.

This perspective was dominant in Protestantism, because of the Reformation debates. Many interpreters in the Reformed tradition came to regard Paul's relationship with Judaism as similar to that between Martin Luther and the Roman Catholic Church. Just as Luther battled for the clarity of the gospel of grace in the face of ecclesiastical and magisterial corruption, Paul opposed the corruption of the pure gospel of grace in Judaism.

On this view the Pharisees are regarded as leaders of this legalistic impulse. They regarded themselves as more righteous than the average Jewish person, having memorized Scripture and worked to attain the status of leaders in Israel. They did their works of righteousness before men and they assumed that their status before God was secure because of their good deeds. Paul would have been a model of this sort of legalistic striving during his time as a Pharisee.

This interpretive stream often reads Paul's conversion narrative through the lenses of Martin Luther's experience. The Augustinian monk struggled with his guilt before God until he discovered the gospel of the grace of God. In the same way, until his conversion, Paul was beset by a guilty conscience. While he might have tried to convince himself that he was righteous before God, he was inwardly frustrated that he could not match the righteousness commanded in the Law. On some accounts of this perspective, Romans 7 is Paul's own testimony of what life was like for him before his conversion. In that chapter, Paul laments "I do not do what I want, but I do the very thing I hate!" (v. 15). Further, "I do not do the good I want, but the evil I do not want is what I do" (v. 19). At the end of the chapter, he cries out, "wretched man that I am! Who will rescue me from this body of death?" (v. 24).

Stricken in this condition of guilt before God, Paul is confronted by the risen Christ and brought to salvation. The glorious gospel that he discovers during his early years as a Christian apostle involves no longer having to do works of righteousness to attain merit for acceptance before God. Paul rejects the route of human effort to please God as he comes to understand that salvation comes solely by the grace of God and involves nothing more than faith in Christ. I will show how this "traditional" interpretation of Paul interprets the texts mentioned above.

1.1 Galatians 2:15–21

The statements here are fairly straightforward. Paul means to say that even though he is a Jew he has now come to understand that justification does not come through legalistic obedience to the Mosaic Law, but through trust in Jesus Christ. Therefore, he puts his trust in Christ for justification, since no one can be justified through legalism (v. 16). Paul's reasoning here is built upon an implied premise—a central conviction of Paul's that he nowhere states explicitly. That premise is that no human can possibly obey the Law perfectly. Since everyone sins in one way or another during her or his life, salvation before God based upon legalism is simply unattainable. If a person were to render to God perfect obedience, then theoretically God would justify that person. Since, however, perfect obedience is impossible, justification through legalism is unattainable.

Paul claims in v. 19 that he has died to the Law, having been crucified with Christ. He means that because of his confession of faith in Christ, he no longer seeks to please God by keeping the Law's requirements. He realizes that this is impossible and his former strivings have left him only tired from trying to please God through his own efforts. His sharing in the death of Christ releases him from having to try to keep the Law's perfect standard. Because of his new-found faith, Paul regards Christ's own obedience to the Law as the righteousness whereby God justifies him. That is, during his time on earth, Jesus lived a life of perfect conformity to the Mosaic Law, pleasing God and earning the righteousness needed by all sinners who will come to put their faith in him. Paul's gospel, according to v. 21, does not nullify God's grace; far from it! It magnifies God's grace, in contrast to the legalistic mode of life inherent in Judaism.

Paul's convictions on this issue are summed by the final statement in Galatians 2: "if justification comes through the Law, then Christ died for nothing." Because legalism is a false route to justification, the death of Christ was necessary to bring sinners to God. If legalistic striving were actually effective, then Christ's death was unnecessary, a notion that Paul does not entertain for a moment.

1.2 Galatians 3:10–14

Paul here lays out a series of arguments aimed at fatally undermining a legalistic vision of salvation. In v. 10, Paul states that "all who rely on the works of the law are under a curse." He bases this statement on a quotation from the Law itself, citing Deut. 27:26; "Cursed is everyone who does not observe and obey all the things written in the book of the law." Paul discerns that the Law clearly curses anyone who does not obey *all the things* that are in the Law. That is, anyone who does not render to God perfect obedience, flawless conformity to the Law, stands condemned by God. Therefore, those who are relying upon their legalistic strivings are under God's own curse. Paul's logic is again built upon the implicit notion that no one can render to God the sort of perfect obedience that God demands.

Paul lays out a second argument in v. 11. It should be obvious that no one can be justified before God based on conformity to the Law, since such a path to salvation before God is not even available. The Scriptures themselves say so. Paul here quotes Hab. 2:4; "the one who is righteous will live by faith." That is, God's approved person enjoys life from God based on faith, not through conformity to the Law.

A third argument comes in v. 12. Paul contrasts the dynamic of the Law with that of faith. They contrast absolutely. "The Law is not of faith." Paul quotes from Lev. 18:5 to let the Law speak for itself.

Contrary to the dynamic of faith, "whoever does the works of the Law will live by them." Paul intends this quote to reveal that the Law's dynamic involves "doing," whereas faith involves believing and resisting the temptation to strive to please God through good deeds.

Paul sums up this series of arguments by again speaking of the death of Christ, in which Christ absorbed the curse against sinners. God does not reckon the penalty for sin against anyone who has faith in Christ, since the penalty for sin has been paid by Christ in his death. His death, then, becomes a way of escape out of the conundrum that previously existed under a legalistic system. How could anyone have been saved under a regime in which perfect obedience was demanded? The death of Christ was necessary to open the possibility for sinners to be reconciled to a holy God who demanded perfect fulfillment of the Law.

1.3 Romans 3:21–31

Paul announces that God is now providing salvation apart from legalistic strivings; "irrespective of Law" (v. 21). The righteousness of God comes through faith in Jesus Christ, and this is the only way that humans can be righteous before God. The way of legalism is impossible, "since all have sinned and fall short of the glory of God" (v. 23). Justification comes as a gift, not as something that can be earned (v. 24).

God undercuts human boasting by excluding human effort from salvation. No one can claim to have earned salvation before God because it does not come by works, only by faith (v. 27). Again, Paul states his fundamental conviction, in v. 28: "For we hold that a person is justified by faith apart from works prescribed by the Law."

1.4 Romans 9:30–10:4

This passage is at the heart of Romans 9–11, in which Paul discusses why Israel has largely rejected the gospel of faith in Christ. His larger point is that it does not have to do with God's faithfulness, but with Israel's blindness. In these verses, Paul is explaining why the gentiles have received God's favor while Israel has not. The surprising state of affairs is that the "gentiles, who did not strive for righteousness, have attained it, that is, righteousness through faith; but Israel, who did strive for the righteousness that is based on the Law, did not succeed in fulfilling that Law" (9:30–31). The reason that Israel did not arrive at salvation is simply that that they misunderstood the nature of the gospel of grace. They were caught in a system of legalism that cut them off from the gospel of faith and so did not attain salvation.

Israel has done this out of a kind of a zeal for God, but it is not enlightened zeal (10:2). The righteousness that comes from God is only attainable by faith, and their pursuit of their own righteousness amounts to a failure to submit to God's righteousness. The Law ought to lead people to Christ in that they will inevitably realize their own sinfulness and receive God's grace by faith.

1.5 Philippians 3:3–11

Paul redefines those who are the true circumcision—the "true Jew," God's genuine Israel. God's approved people are not those who put confidence in their own accomplishments, their own legalistic strivings (v. 3). This is the case even though Paul could make a great case that his own merits were pretty impressive. He then lists a number of accomplishments and points of merit that ought to have put him on the inside track with God. Now that he has come to understand that human strivings do not gain one any merit before God, he regards these "as loss because of Christ" (v. 7). Paul realizes that faith in Christ is the only way of salvation, so he regards his past credentials as loss, as rubbish, in order that he might put his full trust in Christ.

This vision of Paul held sway, certainly among Protestants, since the Reformation, when Luther found in Paul's letters the resources he needed to attack the magisterial and practical corruptions of the church. Paul opposed Judaism because of its legalism. The gospel that Paul preached was antithetical to the religious system in which Paul was raised.

2 THE "NEW PERSPECTIVE" ON PAUL

Throughout the last century, and certainly over the last half-century, the "traditional" interpretation of Paul's relationship to Judaism has sustained a devastating assault. Several scholars have raised serious challenges to the above scenario. Earlier in the twentieth century, several Jewish scholars noted that this scenario was based on a Christian vision of Judaism and of Jewish texts. Christian theological categories and Western Christian renderings of salvation were imposed on Judaism and Jewish literature so that the latter were not treated fairly nor rightly understood.

In the middle of the last century, Krister Stendahl questioned the Protestant psychological vision of Paul's conversion.[1] Paul did not suffer from a tortured conscience prior to his conversion, but had a robust conscience. He had no doubts that he was doing the right thing in persecuting the church prior to God's arresting him on the Damascus road. Stendahl argued that Protestants were interpreting Paul through the lens of the tortured introspective conscience in Western Christian theology, stemming from Augustine and running through Luther. Just as these latter figures suffered under the weight of burdened consciences because of sin, so Paul must have felt the same way. This interpretive lens, Stendahl claimed, was responsible for the above understanding of Paul's conversion and for the viewpoint that Paul was attacking Judaism for its legalism.

The decisive blow to the "traditional" view of Paul came in 1977, with the publication by E. P. Sanders of *Paul and Palestinian Judaism*.[2] Sanders argued that the Christian vision of Judaism as a religion of "works-righteousness" and legalism cannot be sustained from the Jewish literature of Paul's day. Such a view can only be sustained by reading later Jewish texts back into the first century. Further, this view fails to recognize that law-keeping in Judaism had to do with "staying in" the covenant, not "getting in" the covenant. That is, God's grace in election is prior to law-keeping, initiating his covenant with Israel. Only then, once God has adopted Israel as his own people, does he require them to walk in his ways, embodied in Torah. Judaism, then, is a religion of grace, not legalism. The provisions within the Law for forgiveness and restoration ought to have made this clear, but even on a fair reading of early Jewish texts, Judaism can hardly be the religion of legalism that Protestant theology has made it.

Paul's opposition of "faith in Christ" to "Law" and "works of Law" must have some other meaning than the setting of God's grace against legalism. Over the last quarter of the twentieth century, Pauline scholars, especially N. T. Wright and James Dunn, took up these insights and began a fresh investigation of Paul's letters.[3] While the last several decades have been extremely creative in Pauline studies, generating fresh insights and a wild variety of perspectives, something of a new consensus has emerged regarding the fundamental opposition of Paul's gospel between "faith" and "Law" or "works."

According to this "new perspective," Paul is not opposing legalism within Judaism, but *ethno-centrism*. That is, he is opposing the latent, but very strong, impulse within Jewish Christianity that God's salvation in Christ is limited to those who are "within the Law," those who are ethnic Jews or who convert to Judaism. The first generation of Christians was almost exclusively Jewish and their cultural memory of the God of Israel involved his work among the people of Israel *alone*. That the resurrection of Jesus from the dead signaled the end of the age was clear, and that this would have involved the salvation of the gentiles in some sense was not a major stumbling block. But that gentiles being included among a radically new people on the same basis as Jews—the historic people of the God of Israel—was not easy to come to terms with. That Paul was called as Apostle to the gentiles meant that he constantly was elaborating the implications of the gospel for the inclusion of the gentiles in the one new people of God.

Paul's life as a Pharisee did not involve legalistic pursuits nor was he an agent of the "thought police," going around Jerusalem and Judea making sure that people were busy accumulating merit as they earned their way to heaven. Paul was consumed by the hope of Israel, the vindication of Israel's God and God's people. He was trying to bring about the resurrection of the dead, the restoration of all things—the day of the Lord. As an activist Pharisee he was busy working to present to God a righteous nation, a holy people, so that God would bring about the climactic day when he judged Israel's enemies and restored Israel to her rightful place of prominence among the nations, freeing her from Roman oppression. Paul was not burdened with a tortured conscience and he was not necessarily a legalist. He was something more of a political activist in a highly religious national context.

When Paul receives the revelation of the Son of God, seeing the resurrected Jesus exalted as Cosmic Lord, he understands that the end of the ages has come and that Jesus is indeed God's Messiah. This does not lead to the insight that salvation is by free grace as opposed to legalism. Paul's insight is that *participation in the age to come is by faith in Jesus, embodied by following Jesus, regardless of ethnic or social identity*. Participation in the age to come does not come by becoming Jewish, nor is it guaranteed to those who are ethnic Jews. Anyone and everyone is welcome into the people of God—whether Jew or non-Jew, male or female, slave or free. This understanding of Paul's preaching works out in the major texts we have mentioned in the following way.

2.1 Galatians 2:15–21

This passage follows Paul's account of his confrontation with Peter in Antioch in Gal. 2:11–14. When Peter had initially come to Antioch, he had been faithfully embodying the Kingdom of God by enjoying table fellowship with non-Jews. This was a big step for Peter, whose main context for Christian existence was in Jerusalem, among other Jewish Christians. Aside from the episode in Acts 10–11, Peter had not faced the issue of gentile inclusion in the people of God on a continual and sustained basis. After the arrival in Antioch of the hardliners from Jerusalem, however, Peter was intimidated and began to separate himself from the gentiles. They would have strongly disapproved of his fellowship with gentiles, so Peter held himself aloof. This hypocrisy was called out by Paul since it was a severe violation, a performance that heralded an alternative gospel—that gentiles must "live like Jews" in order to participate in the Kingdom of God (Gal. 2:14).

In Gal. 2:15–21, Paul continues to draw out the logic of the gospel for Jewish Christians like Peter and himself. Peter and Paul are Jews by birth but they both know that they are not justified before God because of their being Jewish, but only through faith in Jesus Christ (v. 16). Paul equates being Jews in v. 15 with "works of the Law" in v. 16, indicating that "works of Law" means *deeds that are done that set a person off as an ethnic Jew*. Paul is not talking about legalism, but being Jewish, part of the historic people of God, Israel. Paul goes on to say that they both have come to believe in Jesus Christ because of their common understanding that their justification before God is not based on their ethnic identity as Jews but on their confession of faith in Christ. In fact, no one will be justified by doing "works of Law," not because this is legalism, a false way to God, but because one's ethnic identity is simply irrelevant with regard to justification. It is neither here nor there.

This, of course, places Peter and Paul alongside of "gentile sinners" (v. 17). Paul is here playing on racial impulses running through his Jewish culture that fellowship with gentiles would make them "sinners." Is Christ a "minister of sin" by requiring Jews and non-Jews to enter the Kingdom of God in the same way? After all, this does make Jews rub shoulders with non-Jews! No, not at all, says Paul (v. 17). Paul then gives two reasons why it is necessary for Jews like Peter and Paul to locate themselves alongside gentiles, confessing that their membership in the Kingdom of God comes on the same basis as those whom they formerly regarded as "unclean."

In v. 18 Paul says something quite mystifying: "But if I build up again the very things that I once tore down, then I demonstrate that I am a transgressor." Paul is basing his argument on the incompatibility of holding together a confession of faith in Christ with the conviction that gentiles must "Judaize" (become Jews) in order to be justified. Paul, along with Peter, has embraced the gospel of Jesus Christ, which involves the conviction that salvation has a universal scope, encompassing Jews and gentiles in the one family of God. If Paul now goes back and "rebuilds" his former conviction that limits the saving scope to those who are Jewish, then he has become far worse than a "sinner"; he has become a "transgressor" of the Law! How is this so? This is the case because by virtue of his confession of faith in Christ, he is assenting to the fact that he must fellowship with gentiles as co-equals in the family of God—even if the full implications of this are not fully realized. If he then is pressured to affirm that only those who are Jewish can be saved, he finds himself having transgressed that affirmation that he has just "rebuilt." The gospel of Jesus Christ has brought Jews like Peter and Paul outside their former scope of fellowship. They now must embrace gentile Christians *as gentiles*.

A second reason is given in vv. 19–20, where Paul says that he, along with other Jews like Peter, has died to the Law, through co-crucifixion with Christ. Because he is included in the death of Christ, Paul is no longer bound by its restrictions to live like a Jew, or to follow requirements to avoid contact with gentiles. And because Paul has been raised up with Jesus and is fully alive to God, he can participate fully in that new location where Christ is; wherever there are Jews and gentiles fellowshipping together as the newly created people of God. This passage, then, does not have to do with Paul opposing legalism. Paul is elaborating for his fellow Jewish Christians, and for his Galatian readers, how it is that the new moves that God has made in Christ have made ethnic identity irrelevant for the people of God.

2.2 Galatians 3:10–14

In this passage that is critical for Paul's overall argument in this letter, Paul deploys a series of arguments based on Scriptural texts. We must keep in mind that Paul is not making broad statements about the nature of the Mosaic Law in general, nor are these considered reflections on the nature of Judaism as a religion separate from Christianity. Paul's statements in this passage must be read in terms of his goals for his readers facing their situation in Galatia. When Paul uses the terms "Law," "works," and "works of the Law," he is referring very specifically to the choice that is confronting the Galatians—*whether or not to convert to Judaism in order to be justified before God.*

In v. 10, Paul says that "whoever is of the works of Law are under a curse" (my translation). Paul is referring here to those who are of that very conservative group that has arrived in Galatia from Jerusalem that is teaching that gentiles must convert to Judaism to be saved. They likely do not have the approval of James and the Jerusalem leaders, but they have been tracking Paul's steps in attempts to correct his gospel proclamation. By "whoever is of the works of Law," Paul is not referring to all Jews everywhere, but only to this group in Galatia and to any who are giving assent to their teaching and considering being circumcised. Paul claims that they are under a curse and then quotes Deut. 27:26; "for it is written, 'Cursed is everyone who does not remain within all the things written in the book of the Law to do them'" (my translation).

Paul's argument here is very similar to that in 2:18. He is demonstrating the internal incoherence and impossibility of those Christian Jews who are teaching that gentiles must convert to Judaism to be saved. They are under a curse. This is so because they are holding to both a universal gospel and an exclusive gospel. On one hand they are affirming, by virtue of their genuine faith in Christ, that God is saving people without reference to ethnic identity. At the same time they are affirming an exclusive gospel, that one must be a Jew and remain "within the Law" in order to be saved. By virtue of affirming the first conviction they violate the second and fall under the Law's curse, failing to "remain within" all the things written in the book of the Law to do them. Paul's point, however, is purely rhetorical, since in v. 13 he says that Christ has already absorbed the curse of the Law and exhausted its power to curse. Paul is highlighting the internal incoherence of the agitators' teaching in an effort to keep the gentiles in Galatia from converting to Judaism in order to become Christians.

Paul makes a second point in v. 11; "now because no one is justified by Law before God, it is obvious that the righteous will live by faith" (my translation). Again, Paul is not making a broad point about the character of the Mosaic Law in the abstract, but is referring to the choice that confronts the Galatians. He does not want them to convert to Judaism, taking on an identity shaped by the Law, which amounts to taking on a Jewish way of life. This is not necessary and is not at all the way to being set right before God. On the contrary, citing Hab. 2:4, Paul says that God's approved person will have his life from God on the basis of faith, regardless of ethnic identity.

A third argument comes in v. 12, which is often regarded as one text where Paul obviously argues from the perspective of Judaism as legalistic. This is not, however, the case. Paul claims "the Law is not from faith, but the one who does these things will live by them" (my translation). It is a mistake to regard Paul as contrasting the dynamic of faith with the operating dynamic of the Law, as if faith involves believing and the Law has to do with "doing," pointing to legalistic performance. Paul is referring to the crisis in Galatia and the choice that confronts his readers. He is saying that God wants a life of faithfulness from them and to go down the road of taking on Jewish identity is *not* consistent with faith in God. Paul then quotes Lev. 18:5, which is a passage that has a long history throughout the Old Testament and the literature of the early Jewish period. This text is quoted where the Scriptures emphasize God's promise to bless with life those who are obedient to his word. In this situation in Galatia, Paul is saying that they must choose the way of faith, knowing that God will bless them. They must resist the pressure to convert to Judaism and take on a Jewish identity, since this is not consistent with the life of faith to which God calls them.

In vv. 13–14, Paul again demonstrates that there is no need for fear on the part of faithful Jews. Because they are included in the death and resurrection of Jesus, they have been made part of the new creation people of God in fulfillment of the promise to Abraham that he would be the agency of blessing the nations. Their faithfulness to God does not require them to keep themselves separated from gentiles, but rather demands that they enjoy their status as fellow citizens in the Kingdom of God along with them. Jesus Christ has absorbed the curse of the Law and now the new creation people of God is made up of all those who are followers of Jesus regardless of ethnic identity. This passage does not have to do with Paul's condemnation of Judaism, then. He is attempting to convince his readers to resist the pressure to convert to Judaism in an effort to participate in God's salvation in Jesus. Ethnic and social identity have no bearing on one's participation in the people of God, despite the ethno-centric convictions of the missionaries from Jerusalem in Galatia.

2.3 Romans 3:21–31

In this central text in the argument of Romans, Paul is arguing that God's new move in Christ Jesus means that "the righteousness of God has been disclosed" completely "irrespective of Law" (v. 21). Just as in Galatians, Paul is not making a statement about the Mosaic Law in general but is referring to the controversy facing the churches in Rome. Jewish Christians and gentile Christians are having difficulty sharing in the one new people of God without trying to gain some sort of advantage over one another. Paul is claiming that God's new work involves God's setting people right without any reference to their identity as Jews or non-Jews. On the contrary, "the righteousness of God through faith in Jesus Christ" is "for *all* who believe" (v. 21). Paul's repeated use of "all" throughout the first two chapters of Romans emphasizes that *everyone* in the Roman fellowships stands in need of God's salvation and is equally welcome among God's people. No one has any advantage, "for there is no distinction" between Jews and gentiles (v. 22), "since *all* have sinned and fall short of the glory of God" (v. 23). It is not just the gentiles who are sinners—both Jews and non-Jews stand in need of God's grace.

That justification comes "by his grace as a gift" (v. 24) means that all grounds of boasting have been demolished. The boasting Paul refers to in v. 27 has to do with the two groups in Rome seeking some advantage over the other, not the boasting of the legalist in his accomplishments. Such boasting is excluded by a "law of faith." That is, when everyone in the churches reads the Law as Scripture, consulting it in order to foster lives of faith and love for one another, boasting is excluded. But when the Law is utilized to give the Jews an advantage over the gentiles in the Roman churches ("Law of works"), then there is boasting and the discord and disunity in the fellowships is intensified. But such a reading of Scripture has no place for God's people. Justification comes through faith in Christ without any regard to one's ethnic identity, and the Law ought to be read in line with this conviction. No one ethnicity has any priority before God.

In fact, if they do read the Law as a "Law of works" and prioritize one ethnicity over others, God is only a tribal deity and not the Great King over all the earth. Paul asks in v. 29 "is God the God of Jews only?" Paul is drawing upon the central conviction of Israel, that their God is universal sovereign, God not only of Israel, but sovereign ruler of the nations. If God is the God of Jews only, then this is an inadvertent admission that the God of Israel is only sovereign over the tiny patch of land in Judea, not the Great King over all the earth. But this is most certainly not the case. He is God of the Jews and gentiles, which means that the circumcised and the uncircumcised come to God on the same basis; by faith in Christ. Paul once again draws upon a wealth of resources within the Scriptures of Israel to argue for the universal scope of the gospel.

2.4 Romans 9:30–10:4

As I mentioned above, Paul is here explaining why it is that God's salvation has moved to the gentiles while Jews have, for the most part, rejected salvation in Jesus Christ. If Paul is not contrasting Israel's legalistic obedience to the Mosaic Law with the gospel of grace, but rather an ethno-centric impulse with the universal scope of the gospel, how ought this passage be read?

Paul states the conundrum in vv. 30–31; "gentiles who did not pursue righteousness attained righteousness, that is, the righteousness that is from faith; but Israel, pursuing a Law of righteousness did not attain it" (my translation). That is, how is it that the great majority of Jews are not currently participating in the justified people of God, the new humanity in Jesus through whom God is making all things new? Paul answers, literally, "because not from faith but as if from works" (v. 32, my translation). What he means is that the general conviction on the part of those within Israel who have not become followers of Jesus Christ is that they would be participating faithfully among the people of God through cultivation of faithfulness to Jewish social identity. The "stone of stumbling" is Jesus himself and his preaching of repentance and the demand for faith on the part of those within Israel. Again, one's ethnic heritage and identity is irrelevant with regard to justification before God. This became a difficulty for Jews whose heritage as God's people extended into the past for several millennia.

Paul does acknowledge that they do have a zeal for God, but that it is not an enlightened zeal (10:2). They have not submitted to God's righteousness because they are under the illusion that faithfulness to the Law and the cultivation of national purity will bring about participation in God's work of making all things new. This, however, is not a faithful reading of the Law. If they had been formed rightly as the people of God, cultivating a faithful mode of life in genuine obedience to the Law, they would have been led to follow Christ (10:4). Paul is not contrasting a straightforward legalism within Judaism to faith in Christ. He is, rather, opposing the fostering of faithfulness to an ethnic identity (Jewish identity) with faithfulness to Jesus Christ and his new work among Jews and gentiles.

2.5 Philippians 3:3–11

Paul does indeed redefine what it means to be "the circumcision" in this passage, those who are "true Jews," the true people of God. He is not, however, providing a simple contrast between human efforts and trust in Christ. Something a bit more organic to the argument of Philippians is going on here. Paul redefines what it means to be truly part of God's people in v. 3; "For it is we who are the circumcision, who worship in the Spirit of God and boast in Christ Jesus and have no confidence in the flesh." What Paul is getting at here is participating in the resurrection from the dead (v. 11). What gives Paul confidence that he will participate in the resurrection from the dead and be declared "righteous" at the day of Christ?

Paul confesses that formerly he put his confidence in his credentials that established a firm social identity within Judaism. He had thought that the verdict that might be rendered in his social setting was also the verdict that God would render. His credentials within Judaism were impeccable (vv. 4–6). Paul, however, has had a revolution in his vision, coming to understand that what ensures a person a "righteous" verdict at the day of Christ and joyful participation in the resurrection from the dead is conformity to Christ, specifically participation in the sufferings of Christ. Because of this, Paul regards his former credentials no longer as "gain," but as "loss." Because these are privileges that draw him away from finding creative ways to serve others and suffer for the cause of Christ, they are not merely neutral, but obstacles. These things are loss and he regards them as "rubbish" in order that he might conform his own life more to the life of Christ. His aim is to be found at the day of Christ being united to Christ, having a claim to righteousness that does not come from his credentials, which is no claim at all. He wants to present a claim for vindication as righteous based on his faithful life of imitation of Christ (v. 9).

Paul is not, then, opposing legalism as if human effort were the problem. In fact, for Paul a certain kind of human effort is the problem, while another kind of human effort actually gives a person access to the resurrection power of Christ (v. 10). It is not the case that the problem Paul sees is human legalistic effort and the solution is passive trust in Christ. The problem is seeking to establish a solid social credential—even if that is based on deeds that the Law commands—thinking that the verdict rendered by others is the verdict God will render. And Paul's solution does indeed involve human effort—participation in the sufferings of Christ, which means seeking out opportunities to serve others and to expend oneself for the sake of others in the name of Jesus. This sort of participation in the sufferings of Christ is what guarantees one's participation in the resurrection from the dead at the day of Christ, and the verdict of "righteous" from God.

3 SUMMARY AND CONCLUSION

I have rehearsed two broad visions of Paul and his polemics involving "faith" and the "Law." It may be obvious that my own view is that the "new perspective" on Paul has done a far better job of reading Paul faithfully than the "traditional perspective." In those passages where Paul is contrasting "faith in Christ" with "Law," "works," and "works of Law," Paul is not opposing legalism nor legalistic impulses within Judaism, but the ethno-centrism that ran strongly within the first generation of Jewish Christians. God's work among humanity had always focused on the nation of Israel and they had come to conceive of themselves as God's special people *as opposed to the nations.* That is, while according to the Scriptural narrative God had set Israel apart *in order to redeem the nations,* over time Israel came to regard itself as God's favorite, vis-à-vis the nations. Just as Israel had done, God also hated the nations and longed for their destruction.

When it came to the way of Jesus, then, the first generation of Jewish Christians had little trouble regarding Jesus as the Messiah of Israel, the Savior of the Jews. It was another thing altogether to participate joyfully in the radical implications of Jesus' gospel— *embrace of gentiles as fellow citizens in the Kingdom of the God of Israel.* For Paul, God was no longer working within the boundaries of the nation, no longer limiting his saving work "within the Law," within the social and ethnic identity marked out by Law observance. People from any and every nation could call upon God and be justified by faith in Jesus Christ regardless of ethnic and social identity.

So, what is Paul's view of Judaism? It is not easy to say. Because Paul's letters are occasional, what we can say based on his discussions of "faith" and "works of Law" has to do with the basis of membership within God's new humanity. Justification before God and membership among God's people has nothing to do with deeds that mark one out as a Jew or non-Jew. Salvation is based on faith in Christ, regardless of existence as a Jew or non-Jew. Beyond this, we might say that Paul views the Jewish people as the owners of the promises of God to Israel and that God will eventually fulfill those promises by saving "all Israel." Further, Jews are welcomed among the people of God, which is now constituted by all people of faith, Jew and gentile.

Paul has no harsh polemics for "Judaism" per se. His tough rhetoric is deployed only when gentiles are being pressured to convert to Judaism, a move which would send the message that the God of Israel, the God who is the Father of Jesus, is *not* the Great King over all the earth, and that justification is *not* by faith in Jesus Christ. Whereas normally Paul has words of tender affection for his fellow Jews (cf. Rom. 9:1–5; 10:1), and celebrates his Jewish heritage, when his gentile converts are being upset, the angry rhetoric pours forth from the Apostle to the gentiles.

CHAPTER 6

SALVATION: DIVINE AND HUMAN ACTION

The dramatic shifts that have occurred over the last several decades regarding Paul's relationship to Judaism have led to a reconsideration of the mechanics of salvation in his letters. Paul was formerly regarded as articulating his doctrine of salvation in contrast to the *anthropological optimism* in Judaism. By *anthropological optimism* I mean the dominant understanding of Judaism by Pauline scholars, whereby humanity was thought to play a relatively significant role in salvation. Paul's doctrine of justification by faith was formulated largely in opposition to this, emphasizing human inability, the need of divine intervention, and the notion that humans were largely passive in receiving salvation from God as a gift. On this scenario, "faith" is understood largely as mental assent to truths that are revealed about God in Christ and God's work on behalf of humanity. Salvation is received by simple trust in God. As we indicated previously, Paul was thought to be countering the Jewish notion that a person had the capacity to work his way to salvation.

A wide variety of theological perspectives throughout history have also appealed to Paul for support of their configuration of the dynamics of salvation, especially at the several points where human action and divine action meet. The fiery battles between Augustine and Pelagius in the fourth century often ranged over Pauline turf, with Pelagius emphasizing the human capacity and contribution to salvation and Augustine countering with human inability. The heirs of John Calvin fought over these same issues as Arminius emphasized the responsibility of humanity and Calvinists stressed God's initiative in salvation. Again, Paul's texts were the battlefield on which these divergent perspectives met.

And this is no surprise, since Paul seems not only to affirm but to emphasize both human responsibility to act and God's power to save. In certain passages Paul does indeed emphasize that any human self-congratulation diminishes God's glory in salvation. At the same time, if humans do not act in the form of repentance toward God and faith in Christ, they bear responsibility for their judgment. Further, Paul speaks of justification by faith, but then emphasizes that Christians ought to bear in mind a judgment according to works. Again, Paul gives thanks for God's sustaining grace and his power to enable perseverance on the part of Christians while at the same time warning that unless they persevere, his readers will not inherit salvation. These tensions between human and divine action in salvation call for explanation. In this chapter I will discuss these tensions in Paul's letters and demonstrate that while there are several points of paradox in Paul, there are no final contradictions.

1 JUSTIFICATION BY FAITH AND JUDGMENT ACCORDING TO WORKS

As we saw in our previous chapter, Paul argues that both Jews and gentiles are justified by faith in Christ. This is opposed to any notion that justification is on the basis of "works" or "works of Law." Paul says this in a number of places:

> For "no human being will be justified in his sight" by works of the Law, for through the Law comes the knowledge of sin. (Rom. 3:20)

> For we hold that a person is justified by faith apart from works of the Law. (Rom. 3:28)

> For if Abraham was justified by works, he has something to boast about but not before God. (Rom. 4:2)

> yet we know that a person is justified not by the works of the law but through faith in Jesus Christ. And we have come to believe in Christ Jesus, so that we might be justified by faith in Christ, and not by doing the works of the Law, because no one will be justified by the works of the Law. (Gal. 2:16)

Even if we maintain that Paul is not talking about *legalism* when he uses the terms "works" or "works of the Law," it certainly does seem that Paul is speaking about *human action in some sense and to some extent*. These texts seem to suggest that for Paul justification before God involves faith in Christ *and not human action*. This is widely regarded as the essence of Paul's gospel; that God sets sinners right, reconciling them to himself based on their reception of God's gift, their simple trust in Jesus Christ.

This conviction seems at odds, however, with Paul's statements elsewhere in his letters that there will be a judgment based on works. That is, all of humanity will be judged based on their deeds done during their lives, and their entrance into God's eternal kingdom will be based on how they fare in this evaluation. Paul makes several statements to this effect:

> *For he will repay according to each one's deeds*: to those who by patiently doing good seek for glory and honour and immortality, he will give eternal life; while for those who are self-seeking and who do not obey the truth but unrighteousness, there will be wrath and fury. There will be anguish and distress for everyone who does evil, the Jew first and also the Greek, but glory and honour and peace for everyone who does good, the Jew first and also the Greek. For God shows no partiality. All who have sinned apart from the law will also perish apart from the law, and all who have sinned under the law will be judged by the law. For it is not the hearers of the law who are righteous in God's sight, but *the doers of the law who will be justified*. (Rom. 2:6–13)

> For all of us must appear before the judgment seat of Christ, so that each may receive recompense for what has been done in the body, whether good or evil. (2 Cor. 5:10)

> Why do you pass judgment on your brother or sister? Or you, why do you despise your brother or sister? For we will all stand before the judgment seat of God. For it is written, "As I live, says the Lord, every knee shall bow to me, and every tongue shall give praise to God." So then, each of us will be accountable to God. (Rom. 14:10)

These two sets of passages appear to be in quite clear contradiction. How can Paul at the same time affirm that God justifies a person by faith in Christ *and* that a person will face judgment on the basis of deeds performed?

It seems that there is a further inconsistency here, between Paul's words in Rom. 3:20 and the passage in Rom 2:6–13. How can Paul contradict himself within such a short space? He says first that "no one will be justified by works of the Law" and then that it is "not the hearers of the Law who are righteous in God's sight, but the doers of the Law who will be justified." Let us first deal with this problem within Romans and then handle the tension between justification by faith and judgment according to works more widely.

Paul is speaking in Rom. 2:6–13 about something other than what he is referring to in Rom. 3:20–28. As we said in our previous chapter, when Paul says in Romans 3 that no one will be justified by "works of the Law," he is not referring to deeds done by humans in obedience to God, but rather deeds that are done that establish one's social status. "Works of the Law" are those deeds that are done in keeping with the Law that establish one's identity and status among one's fellow ethnic Jews. Paul has in view especially deeds such as circumcision, Sabbath-keeping, and practices of purity connected to the food regulations. Such works might mark a person out as Jewish, but they carry no weight with regard to justification before God, who shows no partiality between Jew and non-Jew.

In Rom. 2:6–13, Paul refers to this sort of behavior as being a "hearer of the Law," and he distinguishes this from *genuine obedience to God*. God will indeed judge each person's work, as he says in 2:6. The standard by which God will judge is conformity to genuine human conduct. The terms Paul uses in v. 7 refer to God's original design for humanity, as we discussed previously. According to Paul's inherited worldview that was shaped by the Scriptural narrative, God created humanity in his image, which for Paul is functional. God had intended humanity to function as God's "glory," a role that humans fulfilled by conducting themselves honorably, cultivating God's good world and behaving toward one another in a way that mimicked the life of God on earth. Paul claims that those who conform to this sort of behavior will be given eternal life by God.

It is important to note that Paul's discussion here has the Roman fellowships specifically in view. He is stressing to his readers that conformity to a social or ethnic norm is irrelevant for final salvation at the day of judgment. The only thing that matters, for both Jews and non-Jews, is conformity to God's project of renewing humanity and remaking creation in and through Jesus Christ.

Alternatively, those who resist God's work of renewing humanity have nothing but judgment to anticipate. "For those who are self-seeking and who do not obey the truth but unrighteousness, there will be wrath and fury" (v. 8). And this applies to both the Jews and non-Jews in the Roman churches. Paul may here be taking up a slogan that was used by the Christian Jews in Rome to establish their place of prominence over the gentile Christians. It may have been that the phrase "to the Jew first and only then to the Greek" was used to support Jewish-Christian claims of superiority. Paul argues that "there will be anguish and distress for *everyone* who does evil, *the Jew first and also the Greek*, but glory and honour and peace for *everyone* who does good, the Jew first and also the Greek. *For God shows no partiality*" (vv. 9–11).

That Paul means to distinguish between the cultivation of loyalty to a social and ethnic norm when he uses the phrase "works of the Law," and that he means to speak of genuine obedience to God when he speaks of "doing the Law" can be seen in Rom. 2:25–29. Paul says that "circumcision indeed is of value *if you obey the Law*" (v. 25). Paul here distinguishes between Jewish identity, on the one hand, and genuine obedience to God on the other. There is indeed value in being part of the historic people of God by virtue of doing "works of Law," marked out here by his mention of "circumcision." But only if that is part of a genuine obedience to the Law, which obviously is something different from "works of Law." Paul then claims that even non-Jews can be considered "true Jews" when he says that "if those who are uncircumcised [gentiles] keep the requirements of the Law, will not their uncircumcision be regarded as circumcision?" (v. 26). Paul is here playing with the term "the circumcision" to point to membership in the genuine people of God, indicating that if gentiles render to God the sort of obedience that he requires in the Law— something beyond mere loyalty to ethnic identity markers—they will be regarded as among the genuine people of God.

Paul claims that "a person is not a Jew who is one outwardly, nor is true circumcision something external and physical. Rather, a person is a Jew who is one inwardly, and real circumcision is a matter of the heart—it is spiritual and not literal." Or, we might say that it is truly holistic to the entire person; it is not just down to what a person does to mark one isolated portion of his body. Such a person receives praise not from others but from God (vv. 28–29).

All this is to say that Rom. 2:6–13 does not contradict what Paul says in Rom. 3:20–28. Having noted that Rom. 2:6–13 does, however, have to do with God granting salvation to a person based on that person's behavior, the tension remains between the passages in which Paul maintains that justification comes "by faith" and that God's judgment of a person is not based on "works" or "works of the Law." What do we make, then, of the apparent contradiction between these two realities?

Several factors will help to demonstrate that there is no final contradiction between justification by faith and judgment according to works in Paul. First, "faith," for Paul is not a matter of simple trust nor mere mental assent. Conceiving of faith as trust or as some-how opposed to human action is a notion that is foreign to Paul, and it has nothing to do with what he means when he speaks of justification by faith. For Paul, faith does not rule out human action, nor is it something that is opposed to human action. Faith is quite closely tied up with human action, but the kind of human action that carries out what God has truly commanded. When Paul says that no one is justified by "works of Law," he is not opposing all kinds of human action, but the kind of action that is done to establish an approved social status, imagining that this holds sway with God. It is the kind of pursuit to which he refers in Rom. 3:29; action that one carries out to receive praise or approval from men, to demonstrate one's status as a "good Jew." Such action does not hold sway with God. God calls for genuine obedience to the Law, and whoever fulfills this, whether Jew or non-Jew, will be justified before God.

Further, Paul's references to the "obedience of faith" form a paren-thesis to his letter to the Roman churches, emphasizing that his gospel calls for active human obedience. In Rom. 1:5, Paul says that he "received grace and apostleship to bring about *the obedience of faith* among all the Gentiles for the sake of his name." His own view of his commission was to bring about *a kind of human action*, the kind that was consistent with God's own faithfulness. At the close of the letter, he speaks of "the revelation of the mystery that was kept secret for long ages but is now disclosed, and through the prophetic writings is made known to all the Gentiles, according to the com-mand of the eternal God, to bring about *the obedience of faith*" (Rom. 16:25–26). In Romans, then, faith does not involve passivity nor mere mental assent, but a kind of action that is consistent with God's own purposes.

The same holds true in Galatians, where Paul does not set "faith" over-against human action, but rather commends a *kind* of acting. He argues with his readers that Jewish identity is neither here nor there with respect to justification before God. That this contention does not amount to any denigration of human action, however, is seen in his repeated formula in Gal. 5:6 and 6:15. He says first that "in Christ Jesus neither circumcision nor uncircumcision counts for anything; the only thing that counts is *faith working through love.*" Repeating the first part of this formula in 6:15, he equates faith working through love with existence in the new creation people of God: "For neither circumcision nor uncircumcision is anything; but a new creation is everything!" Paul lays this down as a rule of faith, proclaiming peace upon all who make up God's new people in Christ: "As for those who will follow *this rule*—peace be upon them, and mercy, and upon the Israel of God" (6:16). It is no longer the case that Jewish identity distinguishes who are the true people of God. Now that the new creation has arrived because of the death and resurrection of Jesus and the sending of the Spirit, the people of God can be identified wherever there is a faithful community flourishing with acts of love.

For Paul, then, faith is active. He is not contrasting human action and human passivity. The contrast between "faith" and "works" for Paul involves *two different kinds of human action.* The behavior that is irrelevant for justification is that which establishes one's place in any social or ethnic group ("works of Law"). The kind of behavior that brings God's praise (cf. Rom. 3:29) is called "faith." It is the basis for God's justification of a person and it is the basis for judgment at the final day. The judgment according to works, then, will involve whether a person carried out works of faith, or led a life of faithfulness characterized by "faith working through love." In this sense, we might say that "works" are the visible component of "faith," since the only way in which faith can be made manifest is through outward actions.

A second consideration to help resolve this contradiction is Paul's emphasis on believers' *union with Christ.* All those who are incorporated into Christ by the Spirit have forgiveness of sins so that there is no need to fear the possibility of condemnation (Rom. 8:1; Col. 1:22). That is, at the day of judgment, when all of humanity appears before God, believers will be considered by God in the same way as God the Father considers his own Son, Jesus Christ. On this basis, then, there can only be a favorable verdict at the judgment. A believer's sins will have been forgiven so that a person's confession that "Jesus is Lord," which can only be made, according to Paul, by the power of God's Spirit (1 Cor. 12:3), will carry that person through the judgment.

Third, the deeds carried out by believers that are the basis of God's judgment are those that are produced by God's own power, thus eliminating the tension between divine and human action. Such deeds are Spirit-enabled and empowered works. In Eph. 2:8–10 Paul claims that God has saved us by his own grace, stressing God's initiative in salvation. At the same time, the manner in which we participate in salvation is "through faith"—by our own participation in the work that God is carrying out in redeeming creation through Jesus Christ. Yet Paul reminds his readers that this can never be the cause of self-congratulation. Salvation "is not your own doing; it is the gift of God." And the decisive factor that moved God to save is not human action, but God's own grace and kindness. It is "not the result of works" (v. 9). Paul again stresses God's initiative and how it is that God has actually prepared from eternity past the good deeds which believers will perform and by which they participate in God's salvation: "For we are his creative work, created in Christ Jesus for good works, which God prepared beforehand that we ought to walk in them" (v. 10, my translation).

There is no final tension, then, between justification by faith and judgment according to works in Paul. These two dynamics are actually synonymous in that the outward and visible component of faith is a life of good works done in love. The basis of justification before God is faith, the kind of faith that does works of love. And the basis of judgment will be our works, those deeds done in love that are the demonstration of faith. And since, according to Paul, the patterns of goodness in which believers now live are the product of God's own creative and energizing Spirit, the final judgment of believers by God is the examination of the deeds God himself has produced in the lives and communities of Jesus-followers.

2 "FAITH IN CHRIST" OR "FAITHFULNESS OF CHRIST"

A major debate in Pauline studies that gets to the heart of the tensions between the divine and human factors in salvation is the interpretation of the Greek phrase *pistis Christou*, along with similar and related phrases. These expressions appear at crucial points in Romans, Galatians, Philippians, and Ephesians. This phrase is what is called a genitive construction, and it normally would be translated "faith of Christ," or "faithfulness of Christ." In this sense, it is a "subjective genitive," stressing the faith of the subject mentioned in the phrase. Because it sounds odd to be speaking of the faith that Christ exercised, many translations of the New Testament render the phrase as "faith in Christ," stressing the faith on the part of believers in the provision of God in Christ. In this sense, the phrase is an objective genitive, stressing the faith that has Christ as its object. Several of the major disputed passages are here cited with the phrases translated both ways:

We ourselves are Jews by birth and not Gentile sinners; yet we know that a person is justified not by the works of the law but through *faith in Christ / the faithfulness of Christ*. And we have come to believe in Christ Jesus, so that we might be justified by *faith in Christ / the faithfulness of Christ*, and not by doing the works of the law, because no one will be justified by the works of the law. (Gal. 2:15–16)

I have been crucified with Christ; and it is no longer I who live, but it is Christ who lives in me. And the life I now live in the flesh I live by *faith in the Son of God / the faithfulness of the Son of God*, who loved me and gave himself for me. (Gal. 2:20)

But now, irrespective of law, the righteousness of God has been disclosed, and is attested by the law and the prophets, the righteousness of God through *faith in Jesus Christ / the faithfulness of Jesus Christ* for all who believe. For there is no distinction, since all have sinned and fall short of the glory of God. (Rom. 3:21–23)

He did this to show his righteousness, because in his divine forbearance he had passed over the sins previously committed; it was to prove at the present time that he himself is righteous and that he justifies the one who *has faith in Jesus / is of the faithfulness of Jesus*. (Rom. 3:25–26)

For his sake I have suffered the loss of all things, and I regard them as rubbish, in order that I may gain Christ and be found in him, not having a righteousness of my own that comes from the law, but one that comes through *faith in Christ* / *the faithfulness of Christ*, the righteousness from God based on faith. I want to know Christ and the power of his resurrection and the sharing of his sufferings by becoming like him in his death, if somehow I may attain the resurrection from the dead. (Phil. 3:9–11)

This was in accordance with the eternal purpose that he has carried out in Christ Jesus our Lord, in whom we have access to God in boldness and confidence through *faith in him* / *his faithfulness*. (Eph. 3:11–12)

Deciding between these two major options involves a complicated mix of linguistic and theological factors and it is unlikely that any one interpretation is going to gain majority status among scholars over the other. This debate sits directly on top of many of the newer developments in Pauline interpretation, and it becomes something of a crux between competing conceptions of Paul's gospel. It has to do with alternative visions of the relationship between divine provision and human responsibility and also affects Christian proclamation of the gospel.

My own view is that these phrases ought to be read to emphasize the faithfulness of Jesus Christ, his covenant fidelity to God in carrying out his mission as Messiah. Reading these phrases to stress human faith in Christ creates dichotomies where Paul did not intend them. It makes the works/faith distinction one between human action and human passivity, which skews Paul's discussions when it comes to the obedience of faith and the robust human activity involved in faith. Paul nowhere endorses passive reception when it comes to human faith but rather creative, redemptive, and God-empowered action. Further, the objective genitive reading tends to limit faith to mere belief, mental assent, or internal commitment to God. That is, upon hearing the gospel, humans must express belief in the truths that are heard.

But faith, as we have seen, is far more than this, though mental assent indeed is involved in it. "Faithfulness" understood as relational or covenantal fidelity is what Paul means when he speaks of *pistis*. God is faithful, in that he acts from his own covenant fidelity, keeping his promises to reclaim his creation, restore his people, and redeem the nations. The human response of *pistis* is a far more robust notion than even a strong internal commitment to this reality.

The "faithfulness of Jesus Christ," then, is how we ought to regard this and related phrases. Such a reading makes better sense of the passages in which these phrases appear. In Gal. 2:15–16, Paul speaks of human action, specifically his own, along with Jewish Christians like Peter and him, when he says that "we have come to believe in Christ Jesus." But both before and after this statement Paul mentions the opposing alternatives of "works of Law" and "faithfulness of Jesus Christ." It would be redundant for Paul, after just referring to believing in Christ to refer again to "faith in Christ." It makes better sense to regard the opposition in Galatians as between "the faithfulness of Jesus" and "works of Law" in that they are two alternative arenas of existence.

We see this same dynamic in Rom. 3:21–23. "The faithfulness of Jesus Christ" appears just before "for all who believe." It would be strikingly redundant for Paul to speak of "the righteousness of God through faith in Jesus Christ for all who have faith in Jesus Christ." Paul is, rather, stating that righteousness comes through "the faithfulness of Jesus Christ" for all who believe in Christ. Righteousness is not found by cultivating and establishing an identity within Judaism, but rather through participating in the faithfulness of Jesus Christ.

And this is the force of this interpretation for Paul. He had formerly cultivated an identity by faithful behavior within the sphere of Law-shaped existence in an effort to establish a status before others that he hoped would hold sway before God. Now that he has come to see that such an identity is not effective for justification, but that inclusion within the sphere of Jesus' own faithfulness is the way to justification, he has "come to believe in Christ Jesus." This has led, as he says in Gal. 2:20, to his being crucified to his former life and being raised up with Christ so that he is truly alive to God in Christ. And the mode of life that he finds himself caught up into now is the very life of God's own Son. Just as Jesus' own life was a faithful and God-pleasing performance of covenant fidelity, Jesus is now living out that existence in Paul's own life. Paul's life is now directed and empowered by the Son of God "who loved me and gave himself for me."

The subjective genitive reading is significant for reading Paul's letters in the following ways. First, it emphasizes Jesus' own faithfulness as decisive for salvation. For Paul, God's aim is to restore humanity to its original role as God's glory on earth. Jesus lived a life of faithfulness to God, summed up by Paul's statement that Jesus "loved me and gave himself up for me" (Gal. 2:20). As Michael Gorman notes, faithfulness and love, toward God and toward fellow humans, are the essence of covenant faithfulness—the very thing that God is looking for on the part of his renewed people.[1] Jesus, in his faithful life of servanthood, performs that human response to God that God is looking for. This does not close down possibilities for those who are in Christ, as if every human life needs to imitate precisely how Jesus lived. Rather, it opens up possibilities for those who are in Christ. Paul uses the metaphor of the "body of Christ" in several letters in order to speak of how a variety of gifts are necessary to participate in the communal life of Jesus on earth.

In this sense, Jesus' faithfulness to God is a forerunner of the vision of salvation articulated by Irenaeus in the second century. Irenaeus spoke of "recapitulation," by which he meant Jesus' taking up the failed human project and redeeming human existence. Those who are in Christ by the Spirit can now live within this redeemed humanity because of what God has done in Christ.

Second, Jesus' faithfulness sets the pattern for Christian behavior. As we have discussed previously, Paul's ethics are founded upon the cruciform character of Jesus' own life, and the subjective genitive reading captures this, too. Paul regularly calls upon his readers to mimic Jesus' fulfillment of the human response to God through faith and love. The self-giving of Jesus in Phil. 2:5–11 is the mode of life that believers are to imitate, as Paul mentions in Phil. 2:1–4. Paul patterns his own life of self-giving and status-renunciation in Phil. 3:2–11, one of the passages in which Paul mentions the "faithfulness of Christ" (v. 9). For Paul, "faith" is not mere belief but has to do with a holistic mode of life on the part of Christian communities, and the pattern for this is Jesus' own faithfulness to God in his self-giving love for others.

Third, this dynamic captures how it is that Christian existence is participation in God's own life; the life of Jesus lived in believers' lives and in believing communities. Paul speaks of this reality in Gal. 2:20 and Phil. 3:3–11. Paul conceives of his own life as being swallowed up within and absorbed into the very life of Jesus. Jesus' own faithfulness invades this broken reality and overtakes Paul's earthly existence, surrounding, upholding, and empowering his life. In this sense, then, Christian existence is seen as participation in the life of God in Christ, keeping in view both human action and divine action. Paul's will and effort are fully engaged, but God's provision is primary, preliminary, foundational, and indispensable. "Faith" in Paul does not rule out human action, nor is it merely the human response to God. It is participation in Jesus' own faithfulness.

Fourth, this vision of Christian conduct keeps the communal component of salvation in view. Paul's gospel proclamation is not, "here are the facts about Christ; affirm and own them in your hearts." Rather, the gospel proclamation is, "Jesus is God's own answer to God's call for humanity to return and be restored to God. This reality is being lived out in communities all over the world. Come and join one and enter into the faithfulness of Jesus as Jesus himself lives that out within a community of Jesus-followers." For Paul, the "body of Christ" is where faithfulness that mimics Jesus' own faithfulness is performed.

The appearance of the phrase *pistis Christou*, then, and the rich texture of related ideas that Paul draws together through this, and related, phrases, brings together the divine and human dynamics of salvation. God has initiated his work of salvation by opening up new possibilities for genuine human existence. He has done this by sending his own Son (Gal. 4:4) to embody and perform covenant fidelity, creating new possibilities for participation in genuine human existence by the power of God's Spirit.

3 PAUL AND PERSEVERANCE

We have already noted at various points that for Paul salvation is the work of God in Christ, and that to whatever extent human efforts are involved, God's grace is prior and foundational. Because God's creation is enslaved by Sin, Death, and the Flesh—cosmic characters on the stage—and because humanity cannot save itself, God's gracious initiative to save is a constant theme in Paul's letters. There is a tension, however, between passages that highlight the security of salvation and those in which Paul stresses the necessity of perseverance for salvation. How is it that these two notions can be held together without contradiction? In these texts, Paul stresses God's grace, sustaining power, and the certainty of salvation:

> I am confident of this, that the one who began a good work among you will bring it to completion by the day of Jesus Christ. (Phil. 1:6)

Who will separate us from the love of Christ? Will hardship, or distress, or persecution, or famine, or nakedness, or peril, or sword? As it is written, "For your sake we are being killed all day long; we are accounted as sheep to be slaughtered." No, in all these things we are more than conquerors through him who loved us. For I am convinced that neither death, nor life, nor angels, nor rulers, nor things present, nor things to come, nor powers, nor height, nor depth, nor anything else in all creation, will be able to separate us from the love of God in Christ Jesus our Lord. (Rom. 8:35–39)

For this gospel I was appointed a herald and an apostle and a teacher, and for this reason I suffer as I do. But I am not ashamed, for I know the one in whom I have put my trust, and I am sure that he is able to guard until that day what I have entrusted to him. (2 Tim. 1:11–12)

These texts certainly seem at odds with others that stress the *conditionality* of salvation. That is, that unless the condition of perseverance in continued obedience is met, there is no salvation:

I do it all for the sake of the gospel, so that I may share in its blessings. Do you not know that in a race the runners all compete, but only one receives the prize? Run in such a way that you may win it. Athletes exercise self-control in all things; they do it to receive a perishable garland, but we an imperishable one. So I do not run aimlessly, nor do I box as though beating the air; but I punish my body and enslave it, so that after proclaiming to others I myself should not be disqualified. (1 Cor. 9:23–27)

And you who were once estranged and hostile in mind, doing evil deeds, he has now reconciled in his fleshly body through death, so as to present you holy and blameless and irreproachable before him—*provided that* you continue securely established and steadfast in the faith, without shifting from the hope promised by the gospel that you heard, which has been proclaimed to every creature under heaven. I, Paul, became a servant of this gospel. (Col. 1:21–23)

Several considerations will help us to come to grips with this tension, if not finally to resolve it. First, we must note from the outset that Paul is speaking about salvation itself in these passages and not rewards for Christian service—a judgment above and beyond salvation. One way of softening the hard edges of this discussion is by claiming that all those who make a profession of faith in Christ are guaranteed salvation on the final day. From this perspective, those who "fall away" or fail to persevere will still be saved but they may lose rewards when they face the judgment. This cannot be sustained from a close reading of Paul, however. In Col. 1:21–23, Paul is speaking about being reconciled to God through the death of Christ, and that this blessing—salvation itself—belongs to all those who "continue . . . in faithfulness." In 1 Cor. 9:23, Paul is speaking about sharing in the blessings of the gospel, which involves participation in salvation at the day of Christ. As tempting as it is to eliminate the tension completely by claiming that Paul is merely referring to rewards, such an option does not take seriously the character of these texts and their larger contexts.

Second, it is helpful to recall the "already but not yet" character of salvation that we spoke about in Chapter 3. For Paul, God has acted decisively to save in the death and resurrection of Christ. At the same time, however, the decisive day of Christ is still something for which believers are waiting. Of these two "moments" in the scheme of salvation, Paul regularly emphasizes the second as the factor which ought to motivate Christian obedience. For Paul, then, Christian conversion is not the end of a process after which one can rest in the assurance of the blessings of salvation. Conversion, rather, is the beginning of discipleship in the way of Jesus, both communally and individually, the entrance into an entire way of life. And anyone making a profession of Christian faith must *remain within* this way of life until the day of Christ. If they fail to persevere, or fail to remain in the Christian way, there is no genuine Christian reality present, and one can only expect the prospect of judgment.

He says as much in 1 Cor. 15:1–2, a passage in which he chides his readers for their behavior that indicates that the Kingdom of God is not present among them:

> Now I should remind you, brothers and sisters, of the good news that I proclaimed to you, which you in turn received, in which also you stand, through which also you are being saved, if you hold firmly to the message that I proclaimed to you—*unless you have come to believe in vain.*

Paul raises the prospect that whatever faith has existed among them has actually been to no effect, since their behavior betrays so little Christian reality. In 2 Corinthians Paul again exhorts his readers to take an honest assessment of their behavior to determine if they truly are "in the faith." And he does not give them any false assurance based on their past behavior.

> Examine yourselves to see whether you are living in the faith. Test yourselves. Do you not realize that Jesus Christ is in you?—unless, indeed, you fail to pass the test! I hope you will find out that we have not failed. (2 Cor. 13:5–6)

For Paul, then, continued perseverance in the way of Jesus is the ultimate test of Christian identity. If there has been a conversion to Christian discipleship, this is good. But what matters is the perseverance in the "Way" to the end.

In an autobiographical passage, Paul says that his own goal is to "attain the resurrection from the dead" (Phil. 3:11), indicating that the day of Christ and a favorable judgment at the final assize is the goal toward which Paul is striving. He continues:

> Not that I have already obtained it or have already been made perfect; but I press on to grab hold of it, just as Christ Jesus has grabbed hold of me. Beloved, I do not consider that I have already grabbed hold of it; but this one thing I do: forgetting what lies behind and straining forward to what lies ahead, I press on towards the goal for the prize of the heavenly call of God in Christ Jesus. (Phil. 3:12–14, my translation)

When Paul writes about forgetting what lies behind, he is referring to his privileges and credentials. His vision is fixed on the day of Christ and his own aim is to persevere in faith until the end, so that he may attain the goal for which Christ Jesus grabbed hold of him.

We should note that the confidence Paul expresses in the final salvation of the Philippians is not based on their merely having made a start in the faith, but in their constant and consistent faithfulness from the first day until Paul's writing. In Phil. 1:5, Paul gives thanks "because of your participation in the gospel from the first day until now." Based on this, he can express confidence that God will complete what he has begun. Again, Paul says in

v. 7 that "it is right for me to think this way about all of you because you hold me in your heart, for all of you share in God's grace with me, both in my imprisonment and in the defence and confirmation of the gospel." Paul's confidence is based on the gospel fruit he sees in the Philippians' behavior toward him. Based on this persevering faithfulness, Paul has confidence that God truly is at work among them.

Third, we must also keep in mind that even here—perhaps *especially* in speaking about perseverance—we find constant mentions of divine provision. In the near context to Paul's words in 1 Cor. 15:1–2, Paul speaks about God's empowerment in his apostolic ministry:

> For I am the least of the apostles, unfit to be called an apostle, because I persecuted the church of God. But by the grace of God I am what I am, and his grace towards me has not been in vain. On the contrary, I worked harder than any of them—though it was not I, but the grace of God that is with me. (1 Cor. 15:9–10)

Paul's letter to the Philippians repeatedly touches both sides of this tension without ever resolving it. After speaking about the "master story" of Jesus, Paul turns to exhort his readers:

> Therefore, my beloved, just as you have always obeyed me, not only in my presence, but much more now in my absence, work out your own salvation with fear and trembling; for it is God who is at work in you, enabling you both to will and to work for his good pleasure. (Phil. 2:12–13)

Paul wants his readers to work hard to take on the narrative pattern of Jesus—his humiliation followed by his exaltation. This is something for which they must strive, "with fear and trembling." At the same time, however, this is precisely the mode of life that delivers to the Philippians the power of God, who is at work to direct their desires and energize their efforts.

Paul never resolves this tension. Salvation is of the Lord and God has acted powerfully to "grab hold" of him. Yet, Paul must strive to take on a Jesus-shaped existence and must persevere in faithfulness to the end. So it is all up to Paul, right? No, Paul is completely dependent upon God's empowerment to energize him in perseverance. So, Paul can relax and let God take over, right? No, Paul must persevere and not "grow weary in doing what is right, for we will reap at harvest time, if we do not give up" (Gal. 6:9).

For Paul, then, God breaks into enslaved situations and brings the light of salvation, inviting anyone and everyone to participate in the Kingdom of God, the realm in which is found forgiveness of sins, redemption, and justification. This is also the realm in which the power of God's Spirit is at work to sustain believers until the day of Christ. *At the same time*, however, believers are fully responsible to *remain within* this sphere, to persevere in Christ until the end. If they do not, there is only the prospect of judgment to anticipate.

4 CONCLUSION

The revolution in Pauline studies over the last three decades has sparked a reconsideration of the divine and human dynamics involved in salvation. Because of the great diversity within Judaism in Paul's day it is not very helpful to speak of the extent to which Paul differed from his Jewish heritage. What we can say, however, is that for Paul salvation is a gift from God from first to last. God, moved by his grace, has begun to set creation right in the death and resurrection of Jesus, and by the power of his Spirit. With regard to humanity participating in the age to come, this too comes solely and completely by God's gracious gift. None of this, however, diminishes human responsibility to participate in the work of God. Both human dependence on God's grace and human responsibility to participate in the way of salvation are essential. For Paul, however, the initiative and provision of God are primary and foundational in salvation.

CHAPTER 7

PAUL AND WOMEN

There is hardly a more volatile subject today among a broader readership and in Christian churches than Paul's view of women. In the history of the Christian tradition, both feminists and fundamentalists have claimed Paul as their own. What makes the discussion especially difficult is that passages and statements can be found throughout Paul's letters that point in both directions. Paul can fairly be read as alternatively liberationist and misogynist. In this chapter, then, we will discuss this set of passages and the competing interpretive angles from which they might be read. We will also review a more recent hermeneutical proposal for a contemporary appropriation of Paul's texts for the Christian church.

1 THE LIBERATIONIST PAUL

Many contemporary scholars, and certainly modern feminist biblical scholars, highlight the *liberative* impulses in Paul's letters. That is, Paul's gospel proclaims freedom to those formerly oppressed, along with the full dignity of all humanity in the one new people of God. Paul is the first Christian feminist, advocating for the equal dignity of women and men and equal access to positions of responsibility and leadership in the Christian church. This viewpoint is based on the following lines of evidence.

First, Paul included women in his circle of ministry partners. When he writes to the Roman church(es), he commends and sends greetings to a variety of people, especially his fellow ministers of the gospel. It is instructive, along this line, to read Paul's words in Rom. 16:1–7:

> I commend to you our sister Phoebe, a deacon of the church at Cenchreae, so that you may welcome her in the Lord as is fitting

for the saints, and help her in whatever she may require from you, for she has been a benefactor of many and of myself as well. Greet Prisca and Aquila, who work with me in Christ Jesus, and who risked their necks for my life, to whom not only I give thanks, but also all the churches of the Gentiles. Greet also the church in their house. Greet my beloved Epaenetus, who was the first convert in Asia for Christ. Greet Mary, who has worked very hard among you. Greet Andronicus and Junia, my relatives who were in prison with me; they are prominent among the apostles, and they were in Christ before I was.

This passage indicates that Paul sends this letter to the Roman church(es) in the care of Phoebe, who is likely travelling with a small party from Corinth. She is a church leader from Cenchreae and a patroness of Paul's ministry. Paul mentions that she is a deacon in her church, a situation that resonates well with the qualifications for leadership roles in 1 Tim. 3, where women are allowed to serve in that role. In this passage, Paul mentions deacons in v. 8 and then turns to women in v. 11, apparently including them in that office.

Paul also mentions Prisca and Aquila in Romans 16, who had been co-workers with Paul in Corinth during his second journey (Acts 18:1–3). It is noteworthy that Paul mentions Prisca first, indicating that she played a significant part in their gospel partnership, if not the main role. We may see reflections of their teaching ministry and of Prisca's (also called Priscilla) leadership in their encounter with Apollos, which Luke recounts (Acts 18:24–28):

Now there came to Ephesus a Jew named Apollos, a native of Alexandria. He was an eloquent man, well-versed in the scriptures. He had been instructed in the Way of the Lord; and he spoke with burning enthusiasm and taught accurately the things concerning Jesus, though he knew only the baptism of John. He began to speak boldly in the synagogue; but when Priscilla and Aquila heard him, they took him aside and explained the Way of God to him more accurately. And when he wished to cross over to Achaia, the believers encouraged him and wrote to the disciples to welcome him. On his arrival he greatly helped those who through grace had become believers, for he powerfully refuted the Jews in public, showing by the scriptures that the Messiah is Jesus.

Paul also sends greetings to Andronicus and Junia, both of whom he refers to as "prominent among the apostles, and they were in Christ before I was" (Rom. 16:7). Junia, a woman, is regarded as an apostle of Jesus Christ, and as someone who had been a Christian convert from the beginning of the Christian movement. We cannot say much more about Junia with any degree of certainty, but she may have been part of the original group of Jewish pilgrims from Rome who had traveled to Jerusalem for Pentecost, had been converted as a result of the preaching of Peter and the apostles, and had been part of the founding of the Christian church in Rome. At the very least, however, we can say that she was known to Paul and among the Roman network of churches as "an apostle" and as someone who had suffered for the sake of the gospel to the point of being imprisoned.

Paul's network of ministry partners, therefore, included women, who fully participated in the ministry. There are no indications that they did not share fully in the responsibilities that such ministry would have involved. On the contrary, since Junia is called an apostle and Priscilla is noted as having taken a leadership role in instructing Apollos, it is most likely that Paul's circle of ministry partners was fully inclusive of women.

Second, the primary text for reading Paul on this matter is Galatians 3:28: "There is no longer Jew or Greek, there is no longer slave or free, there is no longer male and female; for all of you are one in Christ Jesus." The distinctions within humanity that formerly indicated a person's value no longer hold sway because of God's work in Jesus Christ. Before his conversion to the way of Jesus, Paul regarded everyone according to their social status, assigning them a value according to ethnicity and gender. No longer is this the case. Now that Christ has come to unite his people, ethnic and gender differences are subsumed under the primary identity of membership in the body of Christ. Because of this, there can be no prioritizing of males or females; roles of responsibility and leadership in the home and the church are available to all. Any moves that denigrate or lessen the value of women are illegitimate.

Third, in several passages in 1 Corinthians, Paul expresses mutuality between women and men, wives and husbands. In 1 Cor. 7:1–4, Paul answers the Corinthians' question about marriage, and he does so in a way that honors both partners equally:

Now concerning the matters about which you wrote: "It is well for a man not to touch a woman." But because of cases of sexual immorality, each man should have his own wife and each woman her own husband. The husband should give to his wife her conjugal rights, and likewise the wife to her husband. For the wife does not have authority over her own body, but the husband does; likewise the husband does not have authority over his own body, but the wife does.

According to Paul, husbands and wives have "authority over" one another's bodies. This is to go beyond merely saying that husbands have "authority over" their wives and ought to be considerate of their needs or desires.

Such mutuality is also apparent in 1 Cor. 11, in Paul's discussion of women praying and prophesying in the church. He says, on one hand, in vv. 8–9, "Indeed, man was not made from woman, but woman from man. Neither was man created for the sake of woman, but woman for the sake of man." He balances this, however, with his words in vv. 11–12: "Nevertheless, in the Lord woman is not independent of man or man independent of woman. For just as woman came from man, so man comes through woman; but all things come from God." Much of what Paul has to say here is quite cryptic and his meaning is debated, but Paul does not prohibit women from speaking in the church. The only provision he adds is found in v. 10: "For this reason a woman ought to have a symbol of authority on her head, because of the angels." He does not refer to a symbol of *subjection*, nor to the fact that such a symbol is of *authority granted* from a husband or male church leader. This does not appear to be the authority of another, but simply of the authority of the woman to pray or prophesy.

Fourth, such mutuality also appears in Ephesians 5, where Paul discusses husbands and wives. He begins this section with an exhortation for everyone in the ancient household to "be subject to one another out of reverence for Christ" (v. 21). This is a command for every member of the three pairs of relationships addressed to submit mutually to one another—wives/husbands; children/parents; slaves/masters. Such submission is similar to that found in Phil. 2:3–4: "Do nothing from selfish ambition or conceit, but in humility regard others as better than yourselves. Let each of you look not to your own interests, but to the interests of others." Paul bases his exhortation on the example of Jesus Christ, who gave up his life unto death in order to be exalted by God. In the same way, believers should consider each others' needs as more important than their own. On this view, the relationships delineated in the household code section of Ephesians detail the manner in which such a mutual submission ought to be carried out.

There are a number of texts that inevitably provide trouble for this liberationist vision of Paul regarding women. First Corinthians 14:33b–36 contains the following:

> As in all the churches of the saints, women should be silent in the churches. For they are not permitted to speak, but should be subordinate, as the law also says. If there is anything they desire to know, let them ask their husbands at home. For it is shameful for a woman to speak in church. Or did the word of God originate with you? Or are you the only ones it has reached?

This text appears to contradict Paul's words in 1 Cor. 11, where women are encouraged to pray and prophesy in the churches. For this reason, and because in some ancient manuscripts these verses appear after 1 Cor. 14:40, some scholars have argued that these verses were not originally written by Paul. They are a later insertion by a copyist into the text of this letter, but not the opinion of Paul himself. This is, however, a minority opinion among Pauline scholars.

Another possible way of reading this text is that Paul is safeguarding the social honor of women, who would have had more limited access to education and among whom there would be greater illiteracy. Because women would have been poorly educated, and because of the threat of embarrassment, Paul counsels them to learn from their husbands at home rather than speaking up in the church. Paul prohibits women from speaking in this context, then, only to preserve their social honor and increase the opportunities for their education. If the women in the Corinthian fellowship were better educated, therefore, Paul would not have given this prohibition.

The Pastoral Letters contain several passages that seem to limit leadership roles to men, relegating women to the domesticate sphere. The passage in 1 Tim. 2:11–15 excludes women from teaching and leading:

Let a woman learn in silence with full submission. I permit no woman to teach or to have authority over a man; she is to keep silent. For Adam was formed first, then Eve; and Adam was not deceived, but the woman was deceived and became a transgressor. Yet she will be saved through childbearing, provided they continue in faith and love and holiness, with modesty.

The majority of Pauline scholars claims that the Pastoral Letters (1–2 Timothy and Titus) were written after Paul's death and represent a retreat from the liberative vision of Paul. In order to provide for the successful institutionalization of the Christian church, it was felt to be necessary to adopt traditional roles for women in the church and home, and the Pastoral Letters cement this vision of gender roles.

Not all scholars take this direction, however. Some claim that 1 Timothy was written by Paul but that it does not represent his teaching on women in all circumstances. That is, Paul is not preventing women from teaching or holding positions of leadership without further qualification. On the contrary, Paul is directing his comments toward specific problems in Ephesus, the city in which Timothy has been appointed as church leader. Paul would indeed permit women to teach normally, as we have already seen. There is, however, a specific reason that Paul prevents women from teaching in this instance, and it involves the presence of divisive elders who have made women their target. Because of the problems that have developed, Paul advises Timothy to take the measure of disallowing the women in the church to teach, since they are propagating the error.

In the end, this liberative vision of Paul is driven mainly by the use of Gal. 3:28 as an interpretive lens for the remainder of what Paul has to say about women in his churches. This programmatic statement, in addition to his inclusion of women in his ministry and the positive commendation of women praying and prophesying in 1 Corinthians, leads many to view Paul as having a generally positive vision of women having equal access to leadership positions in the church and home.

2 THE PATRIARCHAL PAUL

An alternative vision of Paul is that he is a patriarchalist, advocating the subordination of women in the home and church. He is not liberative to any significant extent, but rather is socially conservative, upholding the inferior social status of women in the first century. Most Christian scholars who argue for this reading of Paul claim that he would endorse the full equality of women and men with regard to status before God and as humans, but that he limits certain leadership roles within the Christian church and home to men.

In support of this view are the texts in the Pastoral Letters. Paul limits leadership roles to men in 1 Tim. 2:11–15. In this passage, quoted above, Paul excludes women from teaching or having authority over a man in the church. This is not merely Paul's opinion, since he bases this instruction on the creation account, indicating that this is in the very nature of what it means to be male and female, and is an abiding arrangement within humanity and the relations between the two genders.

Further, Paul argues for a traditional social role for women throughout these letters. He states plainly that women are to participate in the redeemed community through childbearing (1 Tim. 2:15). In Tit. 2:3–5, Paul exhorts women to play a proper role within the household:

> Likewise, tell the older women to be reverent in behaviour, not to be slanderers or slaves to drink; they are to teach what is good, so that they may encourage the young women to love their husbands, to love their children, to be self-controlled, chaste, good managers of the household, kind, being submissive to their husbands, so that the word of God may not be discredited.

Paul's words in 1 Tim. 5:11–14 run along the same lines:

> But refuse to put younger widows on the list; for when their sensual desires alienate them from Christ, they want to marry, and so they incur condemnation for having violated their first pledge. Besides that, they learn to be idle, gadding about from house to house; and they are not merely idle, but also gossips and busybodies, saying what they should not say. So I would have younger widows marry, bear children, and manage their households, so as to give the adversary no occasion to revile us.

This reading of Paul does not highlight the notes of mutuality found in 1 Cor. 11, in contrast to the previous view, but rather those of male headship. In v. 3, Paul says that "Christ is the head of every man, and the husband is the head of his wife, and God is the head of Christ." Further, in vv. 7–9, Paul says,

> For a man ought not to have his head veiled, since he is the image and reflection of God; but woman is the reflection of man. Indeed, man was not made from woman, but woman from man. Neither was man created for the sake of woman, but woman for the sake of man.

Such a hierarchical arrangement of men over women overshadows any notion of mutuality in this larger text.

This resonates with Paul's words in 1 Cor. 14:33–36, in which Paul prohibits women from speaking in the church. In contrast to the liberative view of Paul, the prohibition in 1 Cor. 14 does not contradict his words in 1 Cor. 11, as stated above. In 1 Cor. 11 Paul only allows women to pray or prophesy with a symbol of authority on her head (v. 10), which points to some sort of head-covering that signifies her submission to either her husband or the male leadership of the church. If this provision is met, then women may speak in the church. But if not, they must keep silent.

Further evidence for this vision is found in the household codes of Ephesians and Colossians. In Eph. 5, Paul does not argue for mutuality between husbands and wives. The Greek verb that is translated "be subject" in v. 21, and which governs the entire household code, means "to subordinate." It points to a structure within society that involves a hierarchical ordering. It does not have the more general meaning of "submitting," in the sense of being considerate of the needs of others. Some writers have noted this meaning but claim that because Paul includes a reciprocal note—"be subject to one another"—he is calling for mutuality. Hierarchalists respond, however, by noting that Paul only uses this reciprocal pronoun because he is referring to relationships within the church communities, rather than those with outsiders. Further, as the household code unfolds, it is clear that Paul is not talking about mutually submissive relationships.

This is confirmed by a consideration of the parallel appearance of the household code in Col. 3. In this passage, the instruction given in Eph. 5 is far more concise and to the point. Paul writes: "Wives, be subject to your husbands, as is fitting in the Lord. Husbands, love your wives and never treat them harshly" (vv. 18–19). Whereas in

Eph. 5 the verb is implied when it comes to the relationships between wives and husbands, it is applied only to wives in Col. 3. Further, there are no notes of mutuality in Colossians. Paul exhorts women simply to be subject to their husbands, and for husbands to treat their wives with consideration. Hierarchical relationships are maintained.

According to this reading of Paul, then, the apostle endorses a hierarchy of men over women in the home and in his churches. Feminist biblical scholars recognize this and hold Paul responsible for the subjugation and mistreatment of women throughout the history of the Christian church. Other theologians, on the other hand, recognize this but claim that these hierarchical arrangements ought to be maintained within the contemporary home and the Christian church.

3 A THIRD OPTION

There is no denying that both of these competing impulses are found within Paul's letters and Luke's account of Paul's ministry in Acts. Paul appears both to include women within his sphere of ministry, advocating the full participation of women in ministry, but also to limit the access of women to positions of leadership within the Christian church. How are these to be reconciled? This issue has occasioned fierce debate among Christian churches that regard the New Testament as authoritative. It appears that the only option is the arbitrary choice of setting one group of texts over against the other. But this is not the only option. A way past this stalemate has been forged by a recent movement emphasizing the need to interpret Paul's texts with sensitivity to the historical gap between the first century and our current cultural location. That is, this group of scholars solves the problem through a hermeneutical appropriation of Paul rather than a direct application of this or that set of texts.

This approach sets Paul within the canonical context of the Christian narrative, recognizing that God originally designed for women and men to enjoy relationships of equality. According to Gen. 1:26–27, God made male and female to be the image of God, giving them together the commission to care for creation:

> Then God said, "Let us make humankind in our image, according to our likeness; and let them have dominion over the fish of the

sea, and over the birds of the air, and over the cattle, and over all the wild animals of the earth, and over every creeping thing that creeps upon the earth." So God created humankind in his image, in the image of God he created them; male and female he created them.

According to this view, then, the original design for humanity was for men and women to play complementary roles within creation and for them to share equally in the rule of the earth on behalf of God the creator.

The subordination of women, therefore, is the result of the brokenness of creation. Because of the fall into sin and the corruption of human relationships, women have been treated unjustly. Patriarchal cultural arrangements, viewed from a Christian canonical perspective, are manifestations of cultural corruptions and stand in need of redemption.

This view is also eschatological in that it looks ahead to the restoration of all things, which includes the setting right of relationships of equality. When God returns to restore creation and establish his righteous reign on earth—the Kingdom of God—relationships will be restored and injustices will be set right. The church, in Paul's view, is the place where this reality is being lived out and realized. But the church as the Kingdom of God also partakes of the "already/not yet" aspects of Paul's theology, and this likely serves to explain why it is that these twin impulses are both found in Paul's letters. Paul seems to affirm both the full equality of women and men, along with the egalitarian character of relationships in the church and home. In this he is following the ideal from the biblical narrative, taking his cues from the beginning of the canonical story. But because the Kingdom is not here in its fullness yet, Paul does not push for a radical overthrow of contemporary social structures. Perhaps such a "too much, too soon" approach would have been ultimately destructive. But Paul's ideal, according to this movement, is an egalitarian arrangement.

As a test case for this view, we may consider Paul's instructions using the household code form in Ephesians, a passage that also sheds light on how Paul's ethic might be appropriated in a contemporary context. As we will see, Paul's use of the household code, a form borrowed from contemporary political discourse, is both radically transformative and structurally conservative. This may serve to set a trajectory for subsequent Christian reflection. Further, contemporary Christian appropriation of the entire household code is not as straightforward as it may appear. Let us first consider Paul's usage of the household code in Eph. 5:21–6:9.

This entire section is based on Paul's instruction in Eph. 5:18–21. In v. 18, Paul exhorts his readers: "Do not get drunk with wine, for that is debauchery; but be filled by the Spirit." This passage is often interpreted as an exhortation to individuals—rather than being filled with wine and losing self-control, Paul wants Christians to be controlled by the Spirit. But this passage is not directed at individuals, and it does not have to do with being controlled by the Spirit. Paul is commanding his readers to carry out their identity as the household of God, the place where God in Christ dwells by the Spirit. This is the force of the command to "be filled by the Spirit."

Paul had previously noted that the church is the new temple of God by the Spirit in Eph. 2:21–22, the same phenomenon to which he refers in 1:23, where the church is "the fullness" of Christ. Further, Paul had prayed that God would work powerfully in his people so that they might be "filled" with all the "fullness of God" (3:19). Finally, he had discussed the giving of gifted leaders by Christ for the purpose of the growth of the church unto the measure of "the fullness of Christ" (4:13). Therefore, in his command in 5:18 to "be filled by the Spirit," he is not exhorting his readers to be controlled by the Spirit vis-à-vis intoxication with wine, but rather to actualize effectively their identity as the dwelling place of God in Christ by the Spirit.

How does this look? Paul gives a series of community behaviors to pursue in carrying this out. They are to be a praising community as they worship together, giving thanks to God in Christ for all things (vv. 19–20). Paul's final exhortation in being the dwelling place of God is found in v. 21: they are to order themselves appropriately as a community in the fear of Christ.

Paul then embarks on a long discussion of family relationships. Why does he do this? This section is not necessarily Paul's instruction to nuclear families—or, family units as we think of them. Paul uses a distinct form that is found throughout the writings of ancient political philosophers. When political thinkers spoke about the ideal society, they did so in concrete terms, and they considered the smallest unit of society—the family, which consisted of the three pairs of relationships; husband-wife; parents-children; master-slaves. In his work, *Politics*, written about 335 BCE, Aristotle writes:

> Now that it is clear what are the component parts of the state, we have first of all to discuss household management; for every state is composed of households. Household management falls into departments corresponding to the parts of which the household in its turn is composed; and the household in its perfect form consists of slaves and freemen. The investigation of everything should begin with its smallest parts, and the primary and smallest parts of the household are master and slave, husband and wife, father and children; we ought therefore to examine the proper constitution and character of each of these three relationships, I mean that of mastership, that of marriage. . . , and thirdly the progenitive relationship. (*Pol.* I 1253b 1–14)

In a further passage he again relates the household to the state:

> . . . [E]very household is part of a state, and these relationships are part of the household, and the excellence of the part must have regard to that of the whole. (*Pol.* I 1260b 12)

Areius Didymus (70–10 BCE), makes the same connection:

> A primary kind of association (*politeia*) is the legal union of a man and a woman for the begetting of children and for sharing life. This is called a household and is the source for a city, concerning which it is also necessary to speak. For the household is like any small city, if, at least as is intended, the marriage flourishes, and the children mature and are paired with one another; another household is founded, and thus a third and a fourth, and out of these, a village and a city. After many villages come to be, a city is produced. So just as the household yields for the city the seeds of its formation, thus also it yields the constitution (*politeia*). Connected with the house is a pattern of monarchy, of aristocracy and of democracy. The relationship of parents to children is monarchic, of husbands to wives aristocratic, of children to one another democratic. (*Epitome* II.147,26–148,16)

Paul writes using this very same form, utilizing the same set of relationships as are found in ancient political writings. He is, therefore, writing with much the same purpose—to speak in concrete terms about how the new creation people of God are to function as a social body, a political reality. This passage is more or less a manifesto for a radically new society. Because the household was a microcosm of the entire believing community, it provides a concrete model for how Paul's readers can carry out the command in Eph. 5:18–21 to be "the household of God" (Eph. 2:19). This will, of course, have huge implications for family relationships as they participate in the new creation people of God.

When we compare what Paul has to say with contemporary instances, however, both the radical and conservative character of what Paul has to say becomes clear. First, the new creation people of God is a political community where everyone is treated with justice and dignity. Paul's political vision is radical in that all members of God's new people enjoy dignity and honor as humans, and fully participate in the flourishing of the community. This is quite different from contemporary political visions. In other household codes, the same sets of relationships appear (husband-wife; father-children; master-slaves), but the point of the instruction is for the ultimate comfort of the husband/patriarch. That is, the counsel is directed toward the well-ordered household with a view to how the patriarch would maintain control over every other member of the community. Paul's instruction, therefore, is radically subversive. Where there are hierarchical relationships, Paul addresses the subordinate member first, giving them dignity. They are full participants in the people of God. In contemporary visions of society, these members are not addressed at all. They only appear as objects of control by the patriarch. In God's new people, there is no place for control, domination, manipulation of others, nor exploitation.

In contemporary political visions, the patriarch is seen as the only one who is truly human. Others are denigrated or not regarded as worthy of full dignity. According to Aristotle, because women lack the rational capacity of men, wives must be ruled by their husbands:

Hence there are by nature various classes of rulers and ruled. For the free rules the slave, the male the female, and the man the child in a different way. And all possess the various parts of the soul, but possess them in different ways; for the slave has not got the deliberative part at all, and the female has it, but without full authority, while the child has it, but in an undeveloped form. (*Pol.* 1260a 9–14)

Paul rejects this notion, recognizing the full dignity of everyone in the people of God. Each member is worthy of honor and everyone fully and freely participates among God's renewed people.

Second, God's new society is ordered under the Lordship of Jesus Christ. This is in radical contrast to alternative political visions in which communities have Caesar at their head. According to a Roman political system, a person's social rank determined his worth. If one is closer to Caesar, he has greater value. Such a vision fostered all sorts of mistreatment and injustice. Under the Lordship of Jesus Christ, however, no one has any greater value than anyone else. Paul reminds slave-owners that the Lord Jesus Christ is their mutual master, and they will give an account for how they treat those in such a subordinate position. Further, while they can bribe their way out of trouble caused by their mistreatment of their slaves, they will have no way of escaping the searching judgment of the Lord Christ, who is an impartial judge (Eph. 6:9). The treatment of slaves in the Roman Empire—and throughout history—is horrifying to consider. They had no recourse to justice. In God's renewed people, however, those in vulnerable positions are treated with dignity and care.

Third, in God's household, everyone conducts relationships with love and honor. Again, this is radically different from relationships in alternative political arrangements. Many ancient philosophers recognized that people were badly motivated and relationships needed to function from standpoints of power and manipulation. Those in positions of social or cultural weakness would need to gain a foothold of power through manipulation. If they complied with those in authority, it was only a calculated response to avoid punishment. And those in authority would rule through domination, exploitation, and oppression.

But such relational strategies are ruled out by Paul. He exhorts husbands to love their wives; he commands parents to avoid driving their children to become bitter. This, of course, rules out manipulation and control as means of determining children's behavior. And masters are to resist threatening their slaves. Each member of the people of God is to adopt *cruciform* postures toward one another. If there are relationships of power, then those with a superior position must use their power on behalf of others, not against them. Love and justice are to flow along social networks, not manipulation and exploitation.

In these ways, Paul's social ethic is quite radical, differing markedly from contemporary visions of how society ought to function. These radical impulses are those that set a trajectory among the people of God of justice toward the restoration of egalitarian relationships among women and men. Hierarchical relationships are not the ideal, and though Paul does not call for the overthrow of patriarchy and slavery here, the radical notes within his ethic indicate that he sees his own ethical vision as in continuity with a return of the original ideal of egalitarian relationships.

Such a view of how Paul ought to be appropriated by the Christian church today gains in force when we recognize that a consistent appropriation of the relationships in the household code is highly problematic. For those who maintain a hierarchical vision of marriage as normative for Christian practice today, and claim that egalitarian relationships ought to take the form of marriage in the household code, there is a problem. Would not a consistent appropriation of this passage indicate that we ought also to argue for the legitimacy of slavery, and perhaps a return to slavery? At this point, many modern Christians might balk. This is precisely why many scholars more recently have argued for this hermeneutical way of reading Paul's vision for relationships between women and men.

The church's task, then, according to this view, is to examine the Scriptures to see how the gospel invades a culture and transforms it. We consult how the gospel moved into the first century culture and transformed it. And from this, we gain wisdom to discern how the gospel aims to enter our own culture in order to transform it. For Paul, the radical character of the gospel re-ordered relational dynamics, but it did not always completely upend social structures. Even though Paul's ideal, in keeping with the biblical narrative, was fully egalitarian relationships, he did not force this into cultures where such radical transformation would do more harm than good. Today, however, when this would not be the case, at least in most Western cultural situations, relationships can take a more egalitarian shape, given our almost entirely egalitarian social arrangement.

4 CONCLUSION

The hotly contested debate over Paul's view of women in ministry and in the home will likely continue. There is no getting around the fact that Paul's texts contain both straightforwardly liberative statements, and that his own personal conduct in ministry was inclusive of women. At the same time, however, Paul clearly maintains the structure as he finds it in his ancient cultural contexts. Women played a subordinate role in the home and gathered community and Paul does not overthrow this structure. My own sense is that before we prepare to dismiss Paul as responsible for injustices throughout church history, we consider the extent to which he called for justice and dignity for everyone. Paul's political ethic might be understood as more radically egalitarian once it is compared with roughly contemporary rival visions. Furthermore, before Paul is finally damned as a bigot, it is worth considering the extent to which he may have set in motion an ethical trajectory that satisfies our contemporary craving for justice and the equitable treatment of women.

CHAPTER 8

POLITICS AND RELIGION

If we considered only briefly the relationship between politics and religion in the West, we might identify two impulses. On one hand, these two have been intensely integrated. Religious considerations have inevitably figured heavily in national and international politics, often with disastrous results. A competing impulse is to keep these two absolutely separate. Some national charters are intentionally "secular" in order to see to it that these two spheres of human social involvement never meet.

Understandably, these two impulses look to Paul for justification. Paul has been read by many as inaugurating a religious vision in the pietistic tradition, focused on the cultivation of the private inner life. Paul leaves political matters to the state, being completely unconcerned about them. This general view reads Paul's life and letters accordingly. Alternatively, others view Paul as a political thinker, speaking about the reality of the Kingdom of God and the inauguration of a radically new political order oriented around the death and resurrection of Jesus Christ. In this chapter, I will draw out these alternative views of Paul and argue for a more political reading. I will also describe and assess the recent interpretive movement involving Paul's latent anti-imperial rhetoric.

1 PIETISTIC PAUL

For much of the last two centuries, the dominant reading of Paul was to see him as having little or nothing to do with politics at all. According to this way of reading Paul, Jesus had come as the Messiah of Israel to inaugurate the Kingdom of God. This was, of course, a thoroughly political reality. The long-expected Kingdom promised in the Scriptures of Israel was to be realized among that generation in Palestine. Jesus' mission, however, had failed. He was rejected by his people and put to death. Jesus himself recognized this, saying that, "the kingdom of God will be taken away from you and given to a people that produces the fruits of the kingdom" (Matt. 21:43). The Kingdom, then, remains an unrealized promise. When Paul is called as the apostle of Jesus Christ, his message of salvation involves something quite different from Jesus' proclamation of the Kingdom. Jesus came preaching "the gospel of the Kingdom"—the announcement that the reign of God had begun with his arrival and among his followers. For Paul, however, the gospel proclamation does not involve the Kingdom at all. Because the Kingdom has been kicked into the future, Paul's gospel involves God saving people and creating a heavenly humanity who will at some point populate the Kingdom. Because that reality remains a completely future phenomenon, however, it does not have any political implications. For Paul, salvation referred to a future inheritance. The current responsibility of those who are saved is the cultivation of inner piety.

The main topic of Paul's letters, on this view, is the "Christian life"—the individual's communion with the heavenly Christ who resides within each believer by the Holy Spirit. According to Col. 1:27–29, this "mystery" is the burden of Paul's ministry:

> To them God chose to make known how great among the Gentiles are the riches of the glory of this mystery, *which is Christ in you, the hope of glory*. It is he whom we proclaim, warning everyone and teaching everyone in all wisdom, so that we may present everyone mature in Christ. For this I toil and struggle with all the energy that he powerfully inspires within me.

A number of other passages reflect this same reality. Galatians 2 ends in a rhetorically powerful way, as Paul depicts the new reality brought about by the death and resurrection of Christ—the union of the believer and the risen Christ:

> For through the law I died to the law, so that I might live to God. I have been crucified with Christ; and it is no longer I who live, but it is Christ who lives in me. And the life I now live in the flesh I live by faith in the Son of God, who loved me and gave himself for me.

I do not nullify the grace of God; for if justification comes through the law, then Christ died for nothing. (Gal. 2:19b–21)

This viewpoint utilizes Paul's "works/faith" dichotomy to speak of the goal of the individual Christian. Growing as a Christian will involve less "human striving" and more passivity and reliance upon the Spirit. These two extremes—human effort, on one hand, and reliance upon the Spirit, on the other—are synonymous with "works" and "faith" in the various Pauline discussions. Paul's own testimony, found in Rom. 7, bears this out. This passage is often read as Paul's pre-conversion experience. As a Pharisee, he knew the Law of God well and longed to follow it faithfully. He found, however, that he lacked the capacity to carry out a faithful obedience that would lead to inner satisfaction. In fact, just the opposite was true. Knowing the commandments of God actually provoked greater rebellion within him:

But sin, seizing an opportunity in the commandment, produced in me all kinds of covetousness. Apart from the law sin lies dead. I was once alive apart from the law, but when the commandment came, sin revived and I died, and the very commandment that promised life proved to be death to me. For sin, seizing an opportunity in the commandment, deceived me and through it killed me. (Rom. 7:8–11)

Paul finds that he cannot gain satisfaction through his own strivings, but only through surrender and reliance upon the Spirit through whom Jesus Christ indwells him: "Wretched man that I am! Who will rescue me from this body of death? Thanks be to God through Jesus Christ our Lord" (vv. 24–25).

This desire to cease from his own efforts and attain greater communion with Jesus Christ is found also in Phil. 3:

If anyone else has reason to be confident in the flesh, I have more: circumcised on the eighth day, a member of the people of Israel, of the tribe of Benjamin, a Hebrew born of Hebrews; as to the law, a Pharisee; as to zeal, a persecutor of the church; as to righteousness under the law, blameless. Yet whatever gains I had, these I have come to regard as loss because of Christ. More than that, I regard everything as loss because of the surpassing value of knowing Christ Jesus my Lord. For his sake I have suffered the loss of all things, and I regard them as rubbish, in order that I may gain Christ and be found in him, not having a righteousness of my own that comes from the law, but one that comes through faith in Christ, the righteousness from God based on faith. I want to know Christ and the power of his resurrection and the sharing of his sufferings by becoming like him in his death, if somehow I may attain the resurrection from the dead. (vv. 4–11)

Paul's twin commands in Eph. 5:18 and Col. 3:16 are often read along this line. One of the major keys to the Christian life is the cultivation of the Spirit's presence. Paul, in Eph. 5:18, exhorts his readers to "be filled with the Spirit." In contrast to sinful behavior, they are to cultivate the Spirit's presence in their individual lives. When they do, they will have the power to carry out obedience to God. The results of the Spirit's fullness in the Christian's life are seen in vv. 19–21 of that passage. A synonymous command appears in Col. 3:16: "Let the word of Christ dwell in you richly." In saying this, Paul commends to them meditation on the words of Jesus and the teachings of Scripture. Meditation on the Scriptures is a significant way to increase the Spirit's presence and actualize the power of God.

Paul's chief subject throughout his letters, then, is the Christian life—conceived in terms of the individual. And the aim of the Christian life is the cultivation of the inner person, the communion of the soul with the risen Christ through the Spirit, who lives in each believer. Politics is simply outside the scope of Paul's instruction. Insofar as it is a topic of discussion at all, Paul simply states that politics ought to be left to secular governments. He seems to say as much in Rom. 13:

Let every person be subject to the governing authorities; for there is no authority except from God, and those authorities that exist have been instituted by God. Therefore whoever resists authority resists what God has appointed, and those who resist will incur judgement. For rulers are not a terror to good conduct, but to bad. Do you wish to have no fear of the authority? Then do what is good, and you will receive its approval; for it is God's servant for your good. But if you do what is wrong, you should be afraid, for the authority does not bear the sword in vain! It is the servant of

God to execute wrath on the wrongdoer. Therefore one must be subject, not only because of wrath but also because of conscience. For the same reason you also pay taxes, for the authorities are God's servants, busy with this very thing. Pay to all what is due to them—taxes to whom taxes are due, revenue to whom revenue is due, respect to whom respect is due, honour to whom honour is due. (vv. 1–7)

Faithful Christian conduct involves submission to authorities, but this seems to be as far as Paul goes in addressing Christian political involvement.

2 POLITICAL PAUL

Scholars have recognized more recently that it is nearly impossible to claim that Paul was so little interested in politics. And Paul did not exhibit any hint that he viewed Jesus as failing in his mission to inaugurate the Kingdom of God. On the contrary, Paul is quite intensely interested in politics and he does indeed envision the Kingdom to have arrived in with the death, resurrection, and ascension of Jesus Christ, and the sending of the Spirit. God has gathered together his church—a *political* reality—among whom he is present by his Spirit. Further, God has installed Jesus Christ as Cosmic Lord, a *political* title and function. Paul, then, is a political thinker, and his chief topic is Jesus and the new society he has created in his death and resurrection. In this section, we will draw this out in further detail.

First, Luke portrays Paul as chiefly concerned with the resurrection of the dead, the fulfillment of the hopes of Israel. Paul stated as much during his trial before the Jewish Council in Jerusalem (Acts 23:6). Israel's hope, as we have already seen, involved the restoration of the nation as the Kingdom of God, the pivotal political agent of God's redemption of the nations. God had originally intended the nation to be a holy people who conducted themselves with justice, maintaining *shalom* and enjoying the presence of God among them. Israel, however, failed in this and was sent into exile. But God had promised to gather them from the nations, to return with his Spirit, and to make them into a just nation once again. This vision of salvation and of the fulfillment of God's promises shaped Paul's imagination and informs the way he conceives of Kingdom proclamation. Luke ends his account by indicating that the Kingdom of God dominated Paul's preaching:

> He lived there for two whole years at his own expense and welcomed all who came to him, proclaiming the kingdom of God and teaching about the Lord Jesus Christ with all boldness and without hindrance. (Acts 28:30–31)

Paul, therefore, did not regard Jesus' Kingdom aims to have failed. In Paul's "already but not yet" vision of salvation, the Kingdom has already been inaugurated in the church, though it has not yet arrived in its fullness. The church, the gathered people of God from all nations, is the Kingdom of God on earth, the place where God's presence resides and the realm in which the reign of the Lord Christ ought to be manifest.

When Paul speaks of "salvation," therefore, his language must be interpreted in terms of the Scriptural narrative. When this is done, we see clearly that Paul is speaking about nothing less than the fulfillment of God's promises to create a people for himself. This, of course, is a *political* reality—*polis*, the ancient Greek term for city-state, simply points to a gathered people. The core of Paul's proclamation was "the kingdom of God"—God's new political reality brought into being through the death and resurrection of Jesus Christ.

Second, Paul's ethical vision is not oriented toward individuals, but toward the creation and cultivation of Kingdom of God communities. This can be seen from a consideration of the context of the first passage quoted above:

> I am now rejoicing in my sufferings for your sake, and in my flesh I am completing what is lacking in Christ's afflictions for the sake of his body, that is, the church. I became its servant according to God's commission that was given to me for you, to make the word of God fully known, the mystery that has been hidden throughout the ages and generations but has now been revealed to his saints. To them God chose to make known how great among the Gentiles are the riches of the glory of this mystery, which is Christ in you, the hope of glory. It is he whom we proclaim, warning everyone and teaching everyone in all wisdom, so that we may present everyone mature in Christ. For this I toil and struggle with all the energy that he powerfully inspires within me. (Col. 1:24–29)

Paul suffers on behalf of the church of Jesus Christ, which he serves. And the mystery of which he speaks is that God dwells among the gentiles, not merely among his historic people Israel. God has created a new political reality, a gathered multi-ethnic people made up of both Jews and gentiles, and this was unforeseen in biblical history. This is why Paul calls it a "mystery." The promises to Israel had involved their restoration to become once again a light to the nations, but there was no notion of God dwelling among the nations alongside Israel. This new revelation (the "mystery") is "Christ *among* you (gentiles), the hope of glory." It is not merely that Christ dwells *within* each and every person, with individuals carrying on isolated mystical relationships with the risen Christ through the Spirit. The Spirit's work involves his presence *among* the corporate body of Christ—the church—the place where God in Christ dwells.

As I argued in our last chapter, Eph. 5:18 is not rightly read as a statement made to individuals. It is directed to the church *as a gathered body*. They are the dwelling place of God and, as such, they are to be faithful to play their roles in effectively being the new dwelling place of God on earth. The command to "be filled with the Spirit," therefore, is an exhortation made to the corporate people of God, in the context of a political manifesto for how God's people are to shape their community life.

Paul's words in Gal. 2:20 do indeed point to the intimacy between believers and the exalted Christ, but this is not to be understood as some mystical reality as an end in itself. The force of this passage in its context involves Paul's argument with Peter in Antioch (Gal. 2:11–21). Peter had been intimidated when some men from Judea had come down to Antioch so that he separated himself from the gentiles in that church. This action was interpreted by Paul as a destructive *political* act. Whereas God has united Jew and gentile as one new people in Christ, Peter's actions indicated that gentiles needed to become Jewish in order to fully enjoy salvation in Christ. His actions created a hierarchy, setting Jews above the gentiles in Antioch, shaming them and creating division in the community.

Paul confronted Peter at this point and argued that both Jews and gentiles are justified before God on the basis of the faithfulness of Jesus, without reference to ethnic identity. And the newly constituted people of God manifest what God has done in Christ through fellowship with one another. But Peter was surrendering to the cultural prejudice that he could not fellowship with gentiles who were outside the Law. Paul's words to Peter in Gal. 2:19–21, therefore, are aimed at explaining how it is that God has included Jews like Paul and Peter in the death and resurrection of Christ so that they can now fellowship fully and freely with gentiles. Both Jews and gentiles are "in Christ," so that to be intimately joined to Christ is to be intimately joined with gentiles. Again, this is a *political* discussion in that Paul is explaining the new corporate reality that has been created through the death and resurrection of Jesus.

Third, Paul uses Kingdom terminology, along with an array of other corporate terms, to describe the reality brought about by God in Christ. In Col. 1:13, Paul says that God "has rescued us from the power of darkness and transferred us into the kingdom of his beloved Son." Paul imagines two realms, and salvation involves our being given a new cosmic location. We are no longer in the realm of darkness but made inhabitants of the Kingdom of God. Paul draws on this idea in Gal. 1:3–5, in his letter opening:

> Grace to you and peace from God our Father and the Lord Jesus Christ, who gave himself for our sins to set us free from the present evil age, according to the will of our God and Father, to whom be the glory for ever and ever.

Believers no longer inhabit the "present evil age," but now inhabit the "new creation" (Gal. 6:15). When Paul uses this language he is referring to the fulfillment of the promises in the Scriptures to restore God's people in the restored creation, when all things would be made new. This involves, of course, a cosmic reality—participation in the reality of the being-restored creation by the power of Spirit. For Paul, this is the fundamental reality about which he speaks, and this involves renewed political behaviors. No longer does ethnic identity determine personal value (Gal. 3:28). Jews and gentiles must accept and love one another because they have been united by the death and resurrection of Jesus Christ.

Paul's use of "new humanity" terminology points toward his political vision, as well. This language, especially as it appears in Ephesians and Colossians, has often been read as referring to the new disposition within individual Christians. This contrasts with the old disposition of individuals, before conversion. Most modern translations have been affected by a Western individualist conception and so have translated Paul's language to refer to "the new self" and "the old self," rather than to the corporate people of God. Yet, when Paul uses this terminology, he is referring to the latter and not to certain dispositions within individuals. We can see this in Paul's discussion in Eph. 4:17–32. In vv. 17–24, Paul speaks of the "new humanity" and the "old humanity," rather than the "old self" and the "new self," as the NRSV translates these terms. Paul exhorts his readers to put off corrupted behaviors and to put on renewed patterns of life. Each of the behaviors he mentions—both positively and negatively—in vv. 25–32 involve corporate practices.

This is anticipated in Eph. 2:13–16, a passage in which Paul speaks for the first time in the letter about the "new humanity":

> But now in Christ Jesus you who once were far off have been brought near by the blood of Christ. For he is our peace; in his flesh he has made *both groups* into *one* and has broken down the dividing wall, that is, the hostility between us. He has abolished the law with its commandments and ordinances, so that he might create in himself *one new humanity* in place of *the two*, thus *making peace*, and might reconcile *both groups* to God in one body through the cross, thus putting to death that hostility through it.

The "new humanity" in Christ draws both Jew and gentile together in God's one new people, the new political reality brought about through the death and resurrection of Jesus Christ.

Fourth, we may consider the titles used for Jesus Christ. Paul calls Jesus "Lord," which is an intensely political claim. Jesus is not only the Messiah of Israel, but the Lord over the entire cosmos, highly exalted over all powers and authorities (Eph. 1:20–22). We will discuss the potential anti-imperial implications of such terminology below, but it is sufficient here to note that Jesus Christ is the *political* ruler of a newly gathered people—*the new creation polis.*

In conclusion, then, Paul is a *political* theologian. He is cultivating a vision for his churches as outbreaks of the Kingdom of God on earth in accordance with his "already/not yet" vision of God's redemption. The promised Kingdom of God has not yet come in its fullness, but it is indeed here in an inaugurated form—in the form of church communities throughout the world. The church, according to this vision of Paul, is the place where God's reign has been initiated. And Paul envisions the church as the alternative people of God, called to embody the life of God in Christ on earth. Paul's teaching, then, is in continuity with Jesus' vision of the Kingdom.

This vision of Paul has been drawn out throughout the previous chapters of this book, so we will not take too long to elaborate upon it. But this is why so many of Paul's commands have to do with corporate behaviors. Paul wants the communities to which he writes to flourish; to enjoy fruitful and life-giving relationships. Conflicts must be resolved and church leaders must confront those who are behaving in divisive ways. The ultimate value for Paul is unity among his Jesus-following communities. For Paul, if communities of the Kingdom of God are not unified, then God's triumph in the cosmic sphere is diminished. But if the communities he has founded can flourish and cultivate practices that reinforce unity, then God's triumph in Christ is magnified. In the end, for Paul, salvation involves God's restoring humanity to flourishing communities under the Lordship of Jesus. This is a supremely *political* reality, though it will undoubtedly not involve "politics as usual."

3 ANTI-IMPERIAL PAUL

A very recent trend in the interpretation of Paul claims that his letters contain anti-imperial rhetoric. Paul, envisioning the arrival of the Kingdom of God with the resurrection of Jesus Christ and the sending of the Spirit, conceives of the church as a political unit that stands over-against the Roman Empire. And the exalted Lord Christ is an alternative to Caesar. Paul's gospel proclamation of Jesus as Lord is a direct affront to the claims of Caesar as lord. A few lines of evidence are marshaled to support this reading of Paul.

First, very similar claims are made about Caesar as are made about Jesus Christ. The following is from an inscription dating to about 9 BCE, celebrating the birthday of Augustus:

The providence which has ordered the whole of our life, showing concern and zeal, has ordained the most perfect consummation for human life by giving to it Augustus, by filling him with virtue for doing the work of a benefactor among men, and by sending in him, as it were, a savior for us and those who come after us, to make war to cease, to create order everywhere . . .; the birthday of the god [Augustus] was the beginning for the world of the glad tidings that have come to men through him . . .

The term translated "glad tidings" in the final line of this inscription is the same term translated "gospel" in the New Testament. This is very similar language to that used by Paul of Jesus Christ in Col. 1. He speaks of the "gospel that has come to you. Just as it is bearing fruit and growing in the whole world" (vv. 5–6). Paul then speaks in exalted terms of Jesus Christ, emphasizing his Cosmic Lordship over all competing cosmic powers:

> He is the image of the invisible God, the firstborn of all creation; for in him all things in heaven and on earth were created, things visible and invisible, whether thrones or dominions or rulers or powers—all things have been created through him and for him. He himself is before all things, and in him all things hold together. He is the head of the body, the church; he is the beginning, the firstborn from the dead, so that he might come to have first place in everything. For in him all the fullness of God was pleased to dwell, and through him God was pleased to reconcile to himself all things, whether on earth or in heaven, by making peace through the blood of his cross. (Col. 1:15–20)

Some scholars claim that Paul is being directly anti-Caesar in his rhetoric at this point. The claims that Paul makes sound as if he is undermining the commonly held notion that Caesar was the embodiment of the gods, and himself divine. Caesar received worship in the well-established emperor cult, and was seen as the guarantor of the Pax Romana—the peace of Rome. Such claims to divinity would be viewed by Paul as idolatrous and a threat to the unique Lordship of Jesus Christ over all other powers. According to this view, Paul's rhetoric flies deliberately in the face of such idolatrous claims.

Another passage where this shows up is in the central Pauline passage concerning the "self-emptying" of Christ:

> Let the same mind be in you that was in Christ Jesus, who, though he was in the form of God, did not regard equality with God as something to be exploited, but emptied himself, taking the form of a slave, being born in human likeness. And being found in human form, he humbled himself and became obedient to the point of death—even death on a cross. Therefore God also *highly exalted him* and gave him the name that is above every name, so that at the name of Jesus *every knee* should bend, in heaven and on

earth and under the earth, and *every tongue* should confess that *Jesus Christ is Lord*, to the glory of God the Father. (Phil. 2:5–11)

Paul writes this letter to a small fellowship in an intensely Roman city—Philippi. The believers are being persecuted in some way, likely by the Roman authorities. Paul's encouragement to them is to persevere in faithfulness despite their suffering. They are also to get along and continue to foster unity among their small community, despite the temptation either to depart or to begin fighting with one another. Paul encourages them with the example of Jesus Christ who gave himself completely, humbling himself to a shameful death as a Roman criminal. But, according to Paul, God is going to dramatically turn the tables. God has exalted Jesus to the position of Cosmic Lordship, and one day every knee will bow and every tongue confess that Jesus is Lord. The not-so-veiled implication here is that Caesar will be among those bowing his knee to the ultimate Lordship of the suffering and triumphant Christ. While Caesar was proclaimed as "lord," even Caesar will one day confess who is truly Lord, along with all of humanity.

This quite recent trend has surfaced a number of new exegetical insights and has reminded interpreters of the political dimensions of Paul's letters. Further, writers who take this view have emphasized that even if a rhetorically anti-imperial reading of Paul is not fully accepted, it is clear that Paul speaks of the church as at least an alternative political reality; distinct from Judaism and its social and political values, and separate from Roman social and political values. The church as the Kingdom of God is a redemptively alternative political body and must orient its social patterns so that it does not mimic the corrupted practices of any surrounding culture. In this sense, those who have emphasized this angle of approach have made a genuine contribution.

Standing in the way of full acceptance of this interpretive trend, however, is the lack of explicit mentions of Caesar or any definitive anti-imperial rhetoric in Paul. In the absence of explicit statements, those who advocate this approach will continue to emphasize broader patterns and hidden scripts within Paul's letters. More work needs to be done along this line of approach to Paul's letters before any sort of definitive word can be spoken as to whether or not Paul is an anti-imperial political theologian.[1]

4 CONCLUSION

Paul is not, however, a mystic, nor does he view salvation in individualistic terms abstracted from the fundamental communal reality of the arrival of the Kingdom of God in the world. For Paul, Jesus' death and resurrection signaled the end of the age. His ascension and sending of the Spirit created the church, which is the Kingdom of God on earth. Salvation, therefore, is a fundamentally political reality. This may, of course, sound frightening to modern ears that are tired of the culture wars and the place of the Christian church in social conflicts. But the new creation political reality is to fulfill the role to which God originally called Israel. The church is to bless surrounding cultures, cultivating *shalom* and its attendant practices of justice and peace-making. Such a political body would be welcome in many cultures. The Christian church has a long way to go in seeking to live up to Paul's vision of the Kingdom of God on earth.

NOTES

3 THE STRUCTURE OF PAUL'S THOUGHT

[1] Christopher Rowland, *The Open Heaven: A Study of Apocalyptic in Judaism and Early Christianity*, London: SPCK, 1982.
[2] J. Christiaan Beker, *Paul the Apostle: The Triumph of God in Life and Thought*, Philadelphia: Fortress, 1980.

4 THE CROSS AND THE SPIRIT: LIFE AS THE KINGDOM OF GOD

[1] Michael J. Gorman, *Inhabiting the Cruciform God: Kenosis, Justification, and Theosis in Paul's Narrative Soteriology*, Grand Rapids: Eerdmans, 2009, pp. 11–13.
[2] Gorman, *Inhabiting the Cruciform God*, p. 16.
[3] Gorman, *Inhabiting the Cruciform God*, pp. 25–9. Richard Bauckham, *God Crucified: Monotheism and Christology in the New Testament*, Carlisle: Paternoster, 1998, p. 46.

5 PAUL AND JUDAISM

[1] Krister Stendahl, "Paul and the introspective conscience of the West," *Harvard Theological Review* 56 (1963), 199–215.
[2] E. P. Sanders, *Paul and Palestinian Judaism: A Comparison of Patterns of Religion*, Philadelphia: Fortress Press, 1977.
[3] See bibliography for a representative list of their works.

6 SALVATION: DIVINE AND HUMAN ACTION

[1] Michael J. Gorman, *Inhabiting the Cruciform God: Kenosis, Justification, and Theosis in Paul's Narrative Soteriology*, Grand Rapids: Eerdmans, 2009, pp. 88–90.

8 POLITICS AND RELIGION

[1] As an example of this sort of work, see Justin K. Hardin, *Galatians and the Imperial Cult: A Critical Analysis of the First-Century Social Context of Paul's Letter*, WUNT 2.237; Tübingen: Mohr Siebeck, 2008.

BIBLIOGRAPHY

Bassler, Jouette M. (2007), *Navigating Paul: An Introduction to Key Theological Concepts*. Louisville, KY: Westminster John Knox Press.

Bauckham, Richard (1998), *God Crucified: Monotheism and Christology in the New Testament*. Carlisle: Paternoster.

Beker, J. Christiaan (1980), *Paul the Apostle: The Triumph of God in Life and Thought*. Philadelphia: Fortress.

Bird, Michael (2008), *Introducing Paul: The Man, His Mission, and His Message*. Downers Grove, IL: IVP.

Bruce, F. F. (1978), *Paul, Apostle of the Heart Set Free*. Grand Rapids: Eerdmans.

Das, A. Andrew (2003), *Paul and the Jews*. Peabody, MA: Hendrickson.

Dunn, James D. G. (1990), "The new perspective on Paul," in *Jesus, Paul, and the Law: Studies in Mark and Galatians*. Louisville, KY: Westminster John Knox, pp. 183–214.

—(1998), *The Theology of Paul the Apostle*. Grand Rapids: Eerdmans.

Dunn, James D. G. (ed.) (2003), *The Cambridge Companion to St. Paul*. Cambridge: Cambridge University Press.

Elliott, Neil (2006), *Liberating Paul: The Justice of God and the Politics of the Apostle*. Minneapolis: Fortress Press.

Gorman, Michael J. (2001), *Cruciformity: Paul's Narrative Spirituality of the Cross*. Grand Rapids: Eerdmans.

—(2004), *Apostle of the Crucified Lord: A Theological Introduction to Paul and His Letters*. Grand Rapids: Eerdmans.

—(2008), *Reading Paul*. Eugene, OR: Cascade Books.

—(2009), *Inhabiting the Cruciform God: Kenosis, Justification, and Theosis in Paul's Narrative Soteriology*. Grand Rapids: Eerdmans.

Hardin, Justin K. (2008), *Galatians and the Imperial Cult: A Critical Analysis of the First-Century Social Context of Paul's Letter*. WUNT 2.237; Tübingen: Mohr Siebeck.

Harink, Douglas (2003), *Paul Among the Postliberals: Pauline Theology Beyond Christendom and Modernity*. Grand Rapids: Brazos.

Horrell, David G. (2006), *An Introduction to the Study of Paul* (2nd edn). London: T & T Clark.

Horsley, R. A. (1997), *Paul and Empire* (ed.). Harrisburg, PA: Trinity Press International.

—(2004), *Paul the Roman Imperial Order* (ed.). Harrisburg, PA: Trinity Press International.

Longenecker, Bruce W. (1998), *The Triumph of Abraham's God: The Transformation of Identity in Galatians*. Nashville: Abingdon.

Murphy-O'Connor, Jerome (1996), *Paul: A Critical Life*. New York: Oxford University Press.

Perriman, Andrew (1998), *Speaking of Women: Interpreting Paul*. Leicester: Apollos.

Roetzel, Calvin J. (1998), *Paul: The Man and the Myth*. Columbia, SC: University of South Carolina Press.

Rowland, Christopher (1982), *The Open Heaven: A Study of Apocalyptic in Judaism and Early Christianity*. London: SPCK.

Sanders, E. P. (1977), *Paul and Palestinian Judaism: A Comparison of Patterns of Religion*. Philadelphia: Fortress Press.

Schweitzer, Albert (1998), *The Mysticism of Paul the Apostle* (reprint, 1931). Baltimore: Johns Hopkins University Press.

Stackhouse, John G., Jr. (2005), *Finally Feminist: A Pragmatic Christian Understanding of Gender*. Grand Rapids: Baker Academic.

Stendahl, Krister (1963), "Paul and the introspective conscience of the West," *Harvard Theological Review*, 56, 199–215.

Walsh, Brian J. and Sylvia C. Keesmaat (2004), *Colossians Remixed: Subverting the Empire*. Downers Grove, IL: IVP Academic.

Watson, Francis (2007), *Paul, Judaism, and the Gentiles: Beyond the New Perspective* (revised and expanded). Grand Rapids: Eerdmans.

Westerholm, Stephen (2004), *Perspectives Old and New on Paul: The "Lutheran" Paul and His Critics*. Grand Rapids: Eerdmans.

Wright, N. T. (1978), "The Paul of history and the apostle of faith," *Tyndale Bulletin*, 29, 61–88.

—(1997), *What St. Paul Really Said: Was Paul of Tarsus the Real Founder of Christianity?* Grand Rapids: Eerdmans.

—(2005), *Paul: In Fresh Perspective*. Minneapolis: Fortress Press.

—(2009), *Justification: God's Plan and Paul's Vision*. Downers Grove, IL: IVP Academic.

Zetterholm, Magnus (2009), *Approaches to Paul: A Student's Guide to Recent Scholarship*. Minneapolis: Fortress Press.

SCRIPTURE INDEX

2:3–4	17	2:15–16	107, 109
2:9	17	2:15	90
2:12	17	2:16	84, 90, 100
2:13	17	2:17	90–1
3:17–18	68	2:18	91, 92
4:4	48, 49–50	2:19–21	134–5, 140
4:5	71	2:19–20	91
4:7–12	71–2	2:19	84
4:13–18	72	2:20	26, 54, 107, 109,
5:9–10	59		110, 139
5:10	29, 101	2:20–21	68
5:14–17	67	2:21	85
7:8	17	3:10–14	26, 80–1, 85, 92
7:12	17	3:10	85, 92
7:5	17	3:11	85, 93
7:5–16	17	3:12	85, 93
8:1–5	17	3:13–14	93
8:1–15	58	3:13	11, 92
8:17	17	3:28	4, 26, 119, 122, 140
8:18	17	4:3	50
8:22	17	4:4	111
9:1–4	17	4:5	50
11:3	50	4:9	50
11:30–33	31	4:12–15	14
12:14	17	5:6	26, 105
12:21	17	5:7	25
13:1–2	17	5:10	25
13:–56	114	5:10–12	15
		5:22–26	68
Galatians		5:25	55, 68
1:3–5	140	6:9–10	58
1:3–4	55	6:9	116
1:4	26, 54, 67	6:14	26, 55, 67
1:8–9	15	6:15	26, 105, 140
1:13–17	79–80	6:16	26, 57, 105
1:13–14	8		
1:14	9, 11	**Ephesians**	
1:18	12	1–3	36
2:1–10	12	1:1	36
2:10	58	1:10	36
2:11–21	139	1:12–13	56
2:11–14	90	1:15–19	36
2:14	14, 25, 90	1:20–22	141
2:15–21	80, 84, 90	1:21	36, 52, 60

CPSIA information can be obtained at www.ICGtesting.com
Printed in the USA
LVOW04s2150290415

436667LV00029B/489/P

9 780567 033949